THE JUDAEO-CHRISTIAN TRADITION

SECOND EDITION

J. H. HEXTER

YALE UNIVERSITY PRESS
NEW HAVEN & LONDON

First edition published 1966 by Harper & Row.

Second edition published 1995 by Yale University Press.

Designed by Nancy Ovedovitz, and set in Perpetua type by Keystone Typesetting, Inc. Printed in the United States of America by BookCrafters, Inc., Chelsea, Michigan.

Library of Congress Cataloging-in-Publication Data
Hexter, J. H. (Jack H.), 1910–
The Judaeo-Christian tradition / by J. H. Hexter. — 2nd ed.
p.   cm.
Includes bibliographical references and index.
International standard book numbers: 0-300-04571-9 (cloth)
                                      0-300-04572-7 (pbk.)
1. Judaism—History—To 70 A.D.   2. Christianity—Early church,
ca. 30–600.   I. Title.
BM165.H48   1995
296'.09'01—dc20   94–22138
                                             CIP

A catalogue record for this book is available from the British Library.

10   9   8   7   6   5   4   3   2   1

THE
JUDAEO-
CHRISTIAN
TRADITION

SECOND EDITION

CONTENTS

CHRONOLOGY

9th century   The "opposition prophets": Elijah, Elisha.

ca. 750–550   The "writing prophets": Isaiah, Jeremiah, Ezekiel, the Second Isaiah.

722   Fall of Ephraim to the Assyrians.

586   Conquest of Judah by the Babylonians.

586–539   The Babylonian exile.

538   Cyrus of Persia begins repatriation of the Jews.

ca. 550 B.C.–50 A.D.   The expansion of Judaism in the eastern Mediterranean, Babylonia, Persia, the Hellenistic, and the Roman world.

538–332   Jews under Persian rule. The rebuilding of the Temple.

332–198   Jews under rule of Alexander and his successors.

168–63   Maccabean rebellion and establishment of Hasmonean dynasty, which rules until 63 B.C.

63   Conquest of Palestine by Romans.

37–4   Rule of Herod the Great as king of Judea, by Roman authority.

31 B.C.–14 A.D.   Rule of Augustus Caesar.

6–4 B.C.   Birth of Jesus; crucified in 29 A.D.

ca. 34–64 A.D.   Paul's missionary activity; according to tradition, beheaded at Rome under rule of Nero.

66–73   Revolt of the Palestinian Jews against Rome.

70   Jerusalem destroyed by Titus.

132–135   Rising of the Palestinian Jews against Rome put down.

135   Emperor Hadrian bars Jews from Jerusalem.

135–18th and 19th centuries   Ascendancy of rabbinic Judaism throughout the Diaspora.

235–284   Period of crisis (invasions, plagues, civil wars) in Rome; first systematic persecution of Christians by Roman state under Decius (249–51).

284–305   Rule of Diocletian, last Roman emperor to persecute the Christians systematically and openly.

306–337   Rule of Constantine the Great, a convert to Christianity, who in 313 proclaimed equal rights for all religions, including Christianity, throughout the Roman Empire.

325 The first ecumenical council of the Christian church, meeting at Nicaea.

361–363 Rule of Julian, "the Apostate," who led a pagan reaction and tried to substitute the old Roman religion for Christianity.

379–395 Rule of Theodosius the Great, first emperor to make Christianity the official religion of the empire.

410 Sack of Rome by Alaric.

The World of Judaism and Christianity
2000 B.C. – 100 A.D.

David Riphuth

x

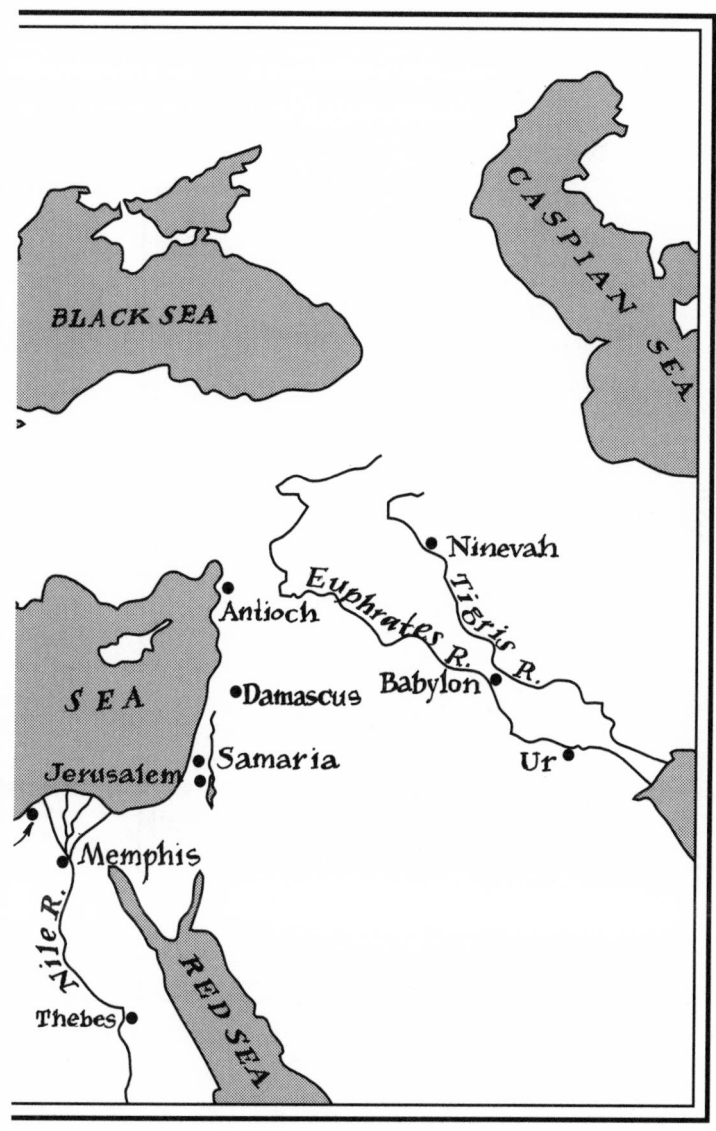

BLACK SEA

CASPIAN SEA

Ninevah

Antioch

Euphrates R.

Tigris R.

SEA

Damascus

Babylon

Jerusalem

Samaria

Ur

Memphis

Nile R.

RED SEA

Thebes

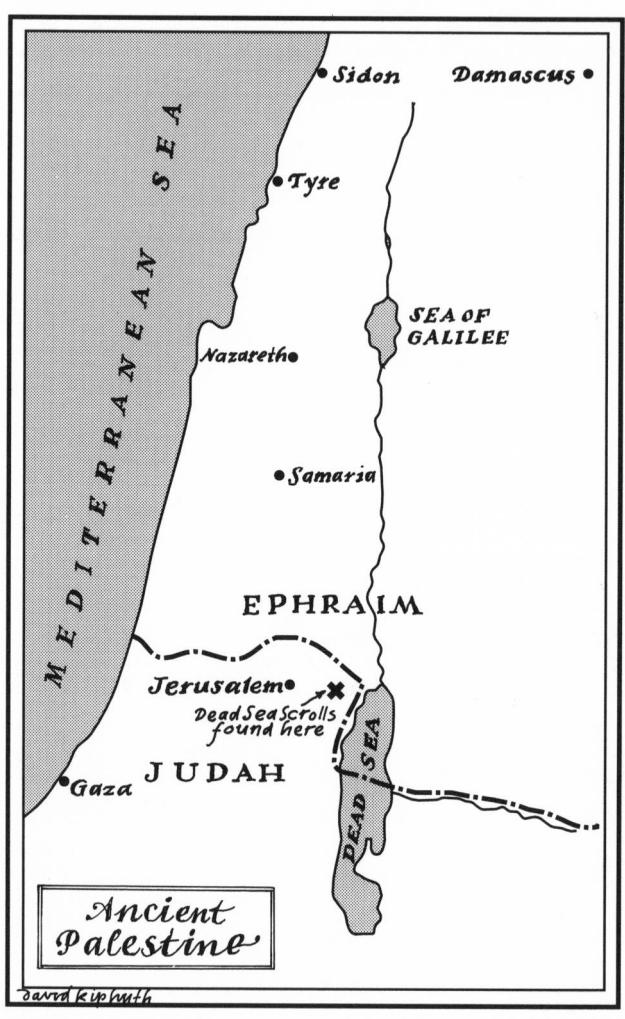

Ancient Palestine

david kiphuth

PREFACE

Every human community whose shared location, or shared purposes, requires its members to do things together in orderly ways has common customs which its common sense requires all its members to conform to. This is as true of the most modern competitive sport, scientific laboratory, or computer game as it is of the most ancient religion. Many such customs are codified into explicit rules, some are learned by those born in the community as they grow up. Such customs often are deeply ingrained over so long a time that they become "second nature" to the members of the community, a tradition to which its members comply without hesitation or doubt or sometimes even thought.

Particular traditions thrive and expand, shrink and wither in the course of history, and change, too, along with the societies that they are actually the traditions of. The oldest living traditions in the world today have to do with beliefs or creeds or religions. And the oldest of all those living religious traditions is the one this little book will be about—the Judaeo-Christian tradition. Only a few tens of years back, one might have unselfconsciously written that the Judaeo-Christian was *the* living religious tradition of the West. But now? A television newsman a few weeks ago casually spoke of "the West—that is, Western Europe, the United States, Canada, and Japan. . . ." Japan? The West?

Geographically no land is less occidental than Japan, and few lands are less Judaeo-Christian in their religious tradition. Yet to describe Japan in the 1990s as "Western" is not nonsense; to describe it as Judaeo-Christian surely would be. Clearly we are at a point in history where our practices of naming are due for an overhaul. Inescapably then, this little volume on a big subject happens to stand at a historical juncture near which there is a good deal of random cultural turbulence. Nevertheless there are few changes in this second edition. I have introduced a brief section at a point where I was too cursory in the first edition of *The Judaeo-Christian Tradition.* The description of the Jewish side of that tradition now ends with a brief account of the span that bridges the return of the exiles from the Babylonian captivity to the effective closure of Judaism from the gentile world after the Roman banning of the Jews of the Diaspora from Jerusalem in 135. This book still stops more than fifteen hundred years short of the present. I have not undertaken to pursue the complex story of the twofold tradition beyond the adoption of Christianity as the sole official cult of the Roman Empire. From then to now that tradition has been a central one of the civilization in which we live. Up to two centuries ago there was no other pervasive religious tradition in the West.

The current turbulence has something to do with the sense of intellectuals in the West that the Judaeo-Christian tradition has not actually opened the gate to the earthly paradise to the human species. It is true that it has not. But then few in that tradition have claimed it as their calling to provide errant mankind with heaven on earth. Some critics have found the Judaeo-Christian tradition, past and present, simply loathsome for the blood on the hands of Christians in the West from the First Crusade until today. Though not always in the name of Christ, the blood has surely been there. In this century, however, prophets of other traditions have claimed to be especially chosen to spill blood, leaders with a special destiny to march or drive the people to the life that history, the leaders said, had promised. Perhaps now Jew, Christian, and non-Christian alike have shed their quota of blood. Perhaps they are ready at last to listen to that part of the Judaeo-Christian message easily lost in the clatter of crusading—the part that calls for repentance and a humble and contrite heart. And perhaps—and most likely—not.

To say a cultural tradition is the oldest in the world is a statement about its durability, not about its worth, at least not directly. The intensity of human appetites, and violence and savagery in seeking to satisfy them, have stained the children of the first human father at least since Cain murdered his brother because Abel's offering found favor with God. Ever since, human beings have borne the mark of Cain. It is not likely, therefore, that any human tradition of considerable durability would continue spotless for very long. Certainly the three thousand years of the Judaeo-Christian tradition did not. It bears the brutal signs of the generations of human beings, all too human, who lived in that tradition for all those centuries, and some of its marks are the marks of the beast. From the beginning or near it, the Judaeo-Christian God was a Lord of Hosts, and He remained a ruler of armies in the nineteenth century and the twentieth of our era. Rudyard Kipling, celebrating the diamond jubilee of Queen Victoria, invoked the "God of our fathers . . . Lord of our farflung battle line." That eloquent bard of more recent crusades may put us in mind that the first Christian Crusade to tear the Holy Places of the Holy Land from the grasp of the Islamic infidel characteristically celebrated its triumph in Jerusalem by massacring the local Muslims with the resident Jews thrown in for good measure. And the crusaders' joy in it puts us in mind of Saul, the first king of Israel who heartily smote the Amalekites and jealously tried to strike down the shepherd-warrior-psalmist David, who succeeded him. So from near the beginning to nearly now the God of Judaeo-Christian tradition has been a Lord of Hosts.

Still there is a bit more to it than that. All dominant traditions are at once exalted and abased by their dominance—some more the one, others more the other. So it seems to me at any rate when I recall the two traditions that in my lifetime explicitly proclaimed their incompatibility with the Judaeo-Christian tradition and declared war on it in the name of the great blessings that their new traditions would bring forth. About half a century ago Adolf Hitler, the German führer, had laid the foundations of the thousand-year Third Reich with conquests that made his Nazi armies masters of Europe from the outskirts of Leningrad, Moscow, and Stalingrad to the Pyrenees. Shortly after that, leaders in the Communist tradition in which atheism was a requirement for orthodoxy held all Europe east of the Elbe except Greece and Turkey, all of Siberia, and all of China. Nearly half of mankind was on the march toward world revolution under the Red flag.

Though fiercely powerful in its first impact, two years after the peak of its power the Nazi Aryan tradition collapsed in rubble, in bloody and disastrous defeat. Today the memorial of the Holocaust, its cold-blooded extermination of European Jewry, is the most visible memorial to Nazism and the Aryan tradition. And the Communist tradition approaches its first century lame, halting, uncertain, with some fifteen million of its own done to death in the Russian Gulag by its great leader Chairman Stalin, and perhaps a like number of millions of Chinese destroyed one way or the other by that other great leader Chairman Mao. So much for the most powerful cultural quasireligious traditions of the past century.

The great long-enduring cultural traditions of mankind—Buddhist, Hindu, Confucian, Muslim, Judaeo-Christian—were, had to be, other than this, although not without their oppressions of others, and when others were in short supply, without exploitation of their own. Still, no culture or religion that survives for hundreds and thousands of years can constantly apply itself to the destruction of those subject to it. Such traditions have to be or to have been in their day in complex and simple ways life-enhancing to their followers—or their followers will cease to follow. So—as we shall see—the God of the Judaeo-Christian tradition was indeed the Lord of Hosts with a terrible swift sword, but he was also the Ever-Loving Father, the Prince of Peace.

ISRAEL

ISRAEL AND THE WESTERN WORLD

Not many years ago, writers on the history of civilization tried to take account of the triviality of Israel's impact on the ancient world. They did so by devoting long chapters to Egypt and Mesopotamia and by burying Israel in a sort of historical pauper's grave—in a few hasty paragraphs between the Hittites and the Phoenicians. From some perspectives on human history such a procedure may be justifiable, but it cannot possibly be justified from the standpoint of cultural history. There is no way of measuring the difference between the relation of Israel to the West and that of ancient Egypt and Mesopotamia. For the difference is not one of measurable magnitude, but of *essence;* the very nature of the relation is different. Ancient Egypt and Mesopotamia survive (or rather have been resurrected) for us in buildings, art, literature, and myth; but the buildings, art, literature, and myths of Egypt and Mesopotamia are *their* buildings, *their* art, *their* literature, *their* myths. Ancient Israel for all practical purposes survives for us only in one book, but that book is *our* Book—literally *The Book*—the Bible. The gods of Egypt and Mesopotamia—Amun-Re, and Horus and Osiris, Enlil and Marduk and Asshur—are dead gods, put on display for us by scholars who have patiently dug them out of their forgotten graves. But the God of Israel is a *living* god, the god who is still worshiped in almost all the churches and synagogues of the West. Today in the West, of course, there are atheists who assert that they do not believe in God, but even they do not quite escape the impact of the God of Israel. The very conception of God that the atheists construct, examine, and then reject is formed on the model of the God of Israel.

There is no continuous link of tradition binding the West to Egypt and Mesopotamia. The ancient civilization of those lands had been virtually forgotten before Western civilization came into being, but an unbroken tradition passes from the ancient Israelites to the peoples of the West. Indeed, the whole spiritual life and most of the earthly claims of the Christian Western world in its early centuries rested on the assertion that it was Israel, the Chosen of God, *the New Israel of the spirit,* the people for whom the God of Israel would fulfill all the promises He had once made to *the old Israel of the flesh.* For Western man, then, the history of the religion of Israel, as distinguished from its secular history, is continuous with the present. But in order to understand that religion, it is necessary first to place the Israelites in their original secular milieu in the ancient Near East during the first millennium before the Christian era.

THE CIVILIZED WORLD, 1500–1000 B.C.

From the sixteenth century B.C. on, it is not possible to consider the civilizations of Egypt and Mesopotamia in isolation. Egyptian and Mesopotamian had already met in the area where both had commercial interests—northern Syria. In fact, by the middle of the third millennium both civilizations had become linked by trade with settled peoples in that area. From their contacts with the higher civilizations of the river plains, peoples all around the Fertile Crescent had learned some of the arts of complexly organized political and social life. Especially they had learned techniques of grain culture, how to concentrate power in well-fortified towns, how to control the countryside from these bastions, and how to establish dominance over weaker urban centers. Among the peoples who acquired the art of state building were the Assyrians of the middle Tigris, the Mitanni of north Syria, and the Hittites, whose center of power lay on the Anatolian (today Turkish) plateau north of the top bend of the Fertile Crescent.

Thus the political powers of the river plains were drawn into a complex network of international relations. Egypt and Lower Mesopotamia had both been overrun in the seventeenth century B.C. Thereafter, to prevent a recurrence of the disaster, the rulers of both areas pursued an active imperialist policy in order to provide defense in depth against their enemies. The Hyksos, who had poured into the Nile Valley by the route through Palestine, had taught the Egyptians that their security depended on control of the line of access from Asia to the Delta, that is, on maintaining a firm grip on the Syrian seacoast. Under the Pharaohs of the eighteenth dynasty, Egypt therefore conquered the coastal cities of south Syria (Palestine or Canaan), established satellite rulers on the thrones of the petty states there, and pushed northward. In north Syria, Egypt had to pursue a complex policy of diplomacy and war to establish a division of power with the three great peoples which, in the fourteenth century, were pressing their aims and claims in the same region—the Mitanni, the Hittites, and the Assyrians. In the thirteenth century a precarious balance of power was established. Egyptians and Hittites, after a long and hard struggle for supremacy, divided control of the western half of the Fertile Crescent, while Assyria spent its military energy in an effort to establish permanent supremacy over the Mesopotamian flood plain.

By the twelfth century, Hittites, Egyptians, and Assyrians all seem to have been exhausted by their earlier efforts. Just as they were at low ebb, the whole area of the Fertile Crescent was struck once again by a mass movement of peoples from the north. By land and by sea, waves of barbarian invaders beat against the old powers of the Crescent. The Hittite Empire was submerged forever. Egypt fought off the invaders from the Nile Delta but was unable to completely maintain its hold in Asia. Assyria had a brief spurt of good fortune at the very end of the twelfth century and then went into another of its recurrent eclipses. Thus it came about that in the eleventh century all the great powers whose policies for hundreds of years had focused on the Crescent from the upper Euphrates to the Peninsula of Sinai were simultaneously paralyzed and rendered impotent to control the course of events in that area. At the same time, the pressure of the invaders slacked off. Because of the power vacuum thus created by the enfeeblement of the great states, lesser folk had a chance to undertake independent state-building in Syria. Some principalities swelled and then burst so quickly as to leave scarcely a trace on the record of history. Others established fairly solid political structures, durable as durability went in that troubled section of the Crescent. But durability never went very far there, and, in fact, all the states that rose out of the decay of the great empires lived on borrowed time. None was able to establish foundations of power broad enough to solidly embrace more than a fraction of the territory that lay between Assyria and Egypt. When one of the great powers managed to get back into action at last (it happened to be Assyria), it toppled the whole flimsy fabric of petty principalities between the Euphrates and the Nile.

All sorts of folk had taken advantage of the respite in great power politics following the eleventh century. Some were old inhabitants of Syria, such as the Phoenicians. Free from Egyptian and Hittite overlords, the Phoenician cities of the central Syrian coast directed their resources seaward. There they found that the former masters of the Mediterranean—the Aegean islanders, among whom the inhabitants of Crete were foremost—had, like the Egyptians and the Hittites, suffered crushing blows from the invading northern peoples. The Phoenicians took advantage of the disaster by spreading their trading settlements along the shores of the Mediterranean. This gave them a virtually un-challenged dominance of seaborne commerce for three or four centuries. To simplify their business documents they drastically simplified their script. Instead of representing whole words and syllables by signs, they represented only the eighteen consonan-tal sounds of their native speech. With modifications and addi-tions these signs have been adopted in all the writing systems now in use in the world except those of the Far East. The Phoenicians had worked out the father of all the alphabets.

Southern Syria or Canaan provided territory for the state-building activities of a couple of newcomers. One group of invaders which had earlier caused so much turmoil in the Crescent, the Peoples of the Sea as they are called in contemporary documents, recoiled from an unsuccessful attack on Egypt and, instead of withdrawing from the area altogether, seized the coastal plain of southern Canaan, gaining a firm hold, especially in the area known today as the Gaza Strip. There they established several city states. These people were called the Philistines; from them the name Palestine, later given to all of Canaan, is derived.

Finally, a number of the seminomadic shepherd folk who for centuries had wandered about the fringe of grazing land along the margins of the Fertile Crescent seized the chance to put down roots in rich country no longer held by the great powers. Among the many incursions of Semitic peoples from the pasture land on to the sown, two were especially successful, that of the Aramaean people, who settled in the region of Damascus, and that of the Israelites, who occupied the hill country of Canaan, east of the coastal lands held by Philistines and Phoenicians. It is with this latter second-rate state—the one established by the Israelites—that we are here concerned.

THE ADVENT OF THE ISRAELITES

As I have said above, the margins of the Fertile Crescent provided enough of a grass cover to sustain a considerable population which lived primarily, not by cultivating fields, but by grazing flocks and herds. While living in relatively intimate contact with the international civilization of the Crescent itself, the nomadic peoples of the highlands were nevertheless backward compared with the more advanced civilizations that lay in a band around them. They had little direct experience of the village community, the city, or the great state which provided social bonds for intricate groupings of men among the more civilized peoples of the Crescent. These groupings were conditioned by long occupation of the land and an equally long tradition of cultivation of the fields. The principal bond of the nomadic peoples was blood and a tradition of descent from a common ancestor; their organization was not territorial but tribal. Two or more tribes might amalgamate if their numbers shrank, or one might subdivide if it grew too large, although even in the latter case the separate tribes sometimes kept alive a tradition of their common origin.

Occasionally a coalition of pastoral tribes attempted to take over control of a section of the sown land. In parts of the Crescent there was no sharp line of geographical demarcation between the people of the sown land and those of the pasture land. Especially in dry country without rivers suitable for irrigation, farming cities with their surrounding fields, rising mainly on oases where there was enough water for agriculture, stood like islands amid a shifting sea of pastoral tribes. Like the Bedouins of our day, the peoples of tents and flocks and tribes were distinguished from the peoples of towns and farms, not by geographical boundaries, but by their way of life. Except for the coastal plain, Canaan was a land where scattered farming cities stood in uneasy and often hostile relations with the herdsmen all around them.

During the twelfth century B.C., the cities of Canaan underwent a double assault. The Philistines established themselves on the coastal plain and began to fan out into the interior from the towns in which they had first settled. At the same time, the inland farming towns had to meet a series of attacks from the nomadic bands known as the Israelites. Toward the end of the eleventh century, a decisive struggle took place between the Philistines and the Israelites for the domination of Canaan.

The Israelites of the tenth century B.C. were an economically mixed group of peoples or tribes, some of them settled in farming cities or hill towns earlier seized from the Canaanites, some of them still seminomadic, moving through the pasture land of Canaan with their flocks. But when we encounter the Israelites in the tenth century B.C., they are already possessed of a full canon of tales about their past that stretches far back in time, long before their incursion into Canaan began. Later versions of these tales of the Israelite past fill many pages of the first seven books of the Old Testament. We find them in the Five Books of Moses, and in the Books of Joshua and Judges.

Like the tradition of many similar peoples, transmitted by word of mouth, generation after generation for many centuries, the tradition of the tenth-century Israelites was an extremely intricate mixture of myths, legends, tales of folk-heroes, and historical fact. For years, patient and careful scholars have been studying the mass of Israelite tradition embedded in the first seven books of the Old Testament in an attempt to sift the historical part out of the mingled traditional matrix in which it is deposited. On the whole, however, this painstaking exploration has not resulted in a vast increase in certainty about the history of the Israelites before the tenth century B.C., even though it has considerably shrunk the area of dogmatism. Few people today would argue that the first seven books of the Old Testament contain an unbroken sequence of literal historical facts about the ancestors of the tenth-century Israelites. On the other hand, relatively few, too, would assert that those books are a mere tissue of folk-myth, utterly unrelated to the actual early history, if any, of the Israelites. Although that much consensus has been won in general, there is little or no consensus on particulars. For almost every assertion made by scholars about Israelite history before the time of Samuel, there have been counterassertions made by other scholars that are just about as plausible from the evidence.

In this situation, to tell the real story of the Israelites up to the tenth century is out of the question, since no one is sure what the real story is. Even to tell all the more or less plausible stories is out of the question; it would take too long. Happily it is not necessary to make either choice; there is a third alternative. While we may be very uncertain about the past of the ancient Israelites, the Israelites themselves were not in the least uncertain about it. For the subsequent history of Israel and also for the history of Western civilization it is more important to know what the Israelites thought their past was than to know what it actually was, for what they believed about their past was what almost all their spiritual descendants, both Jews and Christians, with very few exceptions, believed well into the nineteenth century A.D.

According to their own tradition, the Israelites were descendants of a great patriarchal leader named Abraham who had migrated to Canaan with his flocks and his family, all the way around the Fertile Crescent from the region of Ur in Sumer. Abraham had a claim on the land of Canaan, a claim subject to no limitation of time since it was based on a promise that Abraham's god had made to him. Abraham's claim to Canaan had passed from Abraham to his grandson Jacob, the younger son of Abraham's son Isaac. The people of Israel were the descendants of this younger son; they were of the House of Jacob.

While Jacob and his family dwelt in Canaan, his ten elder sons took their stepbrother Joseph, Jacob's favorite, and sold him to slave dealers, who brought him to Egypt. In Egypt Joseph made good, becoming a trusted advisor of the Pharaoh. Being a dutiful family man, he forgave his brothers and brought them all and their families to Egypt to share his good fortune. There, for a long while, the children of Jacob or Israel (as he was also called) and their descendants prospered mightily—somewhat too mightily for the natives, who cherished Egypt-for-the-Egyptians sentiments. After a while (the Biblical narrative itself is rather casual on the chronology of the matter) the older generation died off, and there came a Pharaoh in Egypt "who knew not Joseph." From that time on, the Israelites in Egypt had a bad time of it. The new Pharaoh put the children of Israel in bondage, which may mean only that he exacted from them the sort of work levy that the Pharaohs customarily took from the Egyptians.

The Israelites were unhappy about their new situation, but it was not until a leader appeared in their midst—a leader with the singularly Egyptian-sounding name of Mo Seh, or Moses—that anything was done about it. Despite the Pharaoh's rather strong objections to the loss of so convenient a body of bond labor (he is said to have chased after them and to have gotten drowned in the Red Sea for his pains), the children of Israel, led by Moses, fled from Egypt. Under the guidance of Moses, the Israelites wandered about for a long while in the wilderness—that is, presumably in the Sinai Peninsula and the barren dry country east of Canaan, the present-day Negeb and Kingdom of Jordan. It was during this time of wandering—a period of enforced nomadism after the relatively settled life they had lived in Egypt—that the children of Israel entered into an explicit agreement or covenant with the god Yahweh. They bound themselves to worship him before all other gods and to accept his Law, while Yahweh in his turn made Israel his own special people, his Chosen Ones, and put them under his special protection.

Toward the end of their period of wandering, led by a number of war-leaders called judges, the Israelites began an assault on some of the Canaanite farming cities. They met with varying success. The Philistines were trying to extend their domination over Canaan from the coast, just as the Israelites were trying to extend theirs from the hill towns. Deprived by the feebleness of the Nile kingdom of the aid and protection it had once afforded them, many of the Canaanite towns fell easily to the Philistines. The center of Philistine power lay in the region of the Gaza Strip, that source of bitter contention between twentieth-century Israel and twentieth-century Egypt, and Gaza itself was one of the chief towns of the Philistines. For a time it appeared that the whole population of Canaan—both the farming-city folk and the shepherd people in their midst alike—must fall under the yoke of the Philistines. In the end, however, the Philistines were repelled and contained by the leaders of the Israelites, who became rulers of the whole land around 1000 B.C.

FROM MONARCHY TO EXILE (1000–586 B.C.)

From around 1000 B.C., the secular historical record of the Israelites emerges from the obscurity of mythical reconstruction which characterizes the first seven books of the Old Testament into the relative clarity of legend and fact which characterizes the historical books (Samuel, Kings I and II, Chronicles) properly so called. One school of modern Biblical historians holds that the earliest books were put together long after the decline of the monarchy in such a way as to account for the establishment of the monarchy on the one hand and for its dissolution on the other. The establishment of the monarchy with its characteristic institutions—court, army, a rudimentary bureaucracy, an official priesthood, and the like—necessitated both the keeping of records and the transmission of those records from one reign to another, which could provide the basis for a genuine history. Continual revisions of these records, however, in the interests of particular groups or parties vying for authority in Israel led to their distortion, and to the insertion of what we would regard today as legendary and mythical elements. Nonetheless, such books as Samuel, Kings I and II, and Chronicles contain enough verifiable, plausible, and consistent historical material to allow modern historians, working with the aid of archaeologists, to reconstruct the main lines of Israelite history from the beginning of the first millennium B.C. with some confidence and, in many cases, exceptional accuracy.

In the centuries between the age of the tribal Patriarchs—Abraham, Isaac, and Jacob—and the Philistine invasion, some of the Israelite shepherd people had settled as peasants on the soil of Canaan; this development no doubt was accentuated when by conquest the Israelites had become masters of considerable stretches of farming land in the hill country. Most of the Israelites, however, maintained their older pastoral way of life. It was no small matter to induce these tribes, habituated to an anarchic independence, to act together on a common plan for a common end. Under pressure of danger, however, the tribes surrendered some of their independence and made a fervent war leader named Saul their king in about 1025 B.C. Under Saul the Israelites won several victories both against the Philistines and against desert nomads who had seized on the general confusion to try to move into Canaan. In the end Saul himself met disaster at the hands of the Philistines and died in battle, and his dominion collapsed. Then, after a period of anarchy, David, a lieutenant of Saul, succeeded Saul as king and reunited the Israelites.

David was an extraordinarily successful war leader. Under his command the Israelites decisively defeated the Philistines, confining them to a small cluster of cities in the southern extreme of the Canaanite sea plain. He advanced his rule through the rest of Canaan, not including the Phoenician maritime cities, and made peoples to the north, the east, and the south pay tribute to him. Thus, around the year 1000 B.C., in the period of a few decades, a new and seemingly powerful Israelite kingdom, centered in the recently conquered city of Jerusalem, suddenly attained a supremacy in the whole of south Syria such as no native state had ever before achieved. The rise of the Israelites was the result of the collapse of the great powers that had hitherto dominated the area, and it had a profound effect on the character of the nation as a whole. David's triumphs speeded the process that had been going on for several centuries—the amalgamation of the once nomadic Israelites with the settled Canaanites, the blending of the customs of the two peoples, and the transition of many of the people of Israel from pastoralism with its tribal organization to farming and urban life.

The good fortune of the Israelite kingdom was as brief as it was sudden. In his reign of forty years, Solomon, the son and successor of David, tried to transform the united Israelite confederation into a territorial despotism on the Mesopotamian model, but among the Israelites the tradition and sanctions for a durable and powerful kingship were even feebler than they had been in the Tigris-Euphrates plain. Solomon lost control of several of the tributary peoples who had acknowledged the supremacy of his father, and on his death in about 933 B.C. the united kingdom split in two—a large northern section, Ephraim,[1] and a smaller southern realm, Judah.

For a few hundred years these two petty kingdoms carried on perpetual war with the other trivial principalities of Syria and the trans-Jordan region and with one another. Meanwhile, on the other side of the Crescent, on the middle Tigris, a great power was awakening that would make a mockery of the pretensions of the princelings and kinglets of Syria. The Assyrian was gathering his strength, preparing to "come down like a wolf on the fold." For a few years in the middle of the ninth century, a large confederation of Syrian states, among which Ephraim played a major part, was able to hold the Assyrian power at bay, but toward the end of that century the kings of Ephraim submitted to making tribute payments to the Assyrian rulers. A century later, two desperate and wholly unsuccessful revolts against the Assyrians sealed the fate of Ephraim. Its land was overrun by the Assyrian host; its capital, Samaria, was besieged, taken, and destroyed in 722; and tens of thousands of its people were deported. Thus ended the larger of the kingdoms of the people of Israel. The smaller kingdom, Judah, enjoyed a respite, in part no doubt because of its very insignificance. At the end of the

---

1. In the Bible the Northern Kingdom is more frequently called Israel than Ephraim. The usage is confusing for our purpose, however, since all the covenanted people of north and south alike were still called Israel too. I shall, therefore, use the alternative *Ephraim* for the Northern Kingdom, *Judah* for the Southern Kingdom, and reserve *Israel* for all the worshipers of Yahweh before the Babylonian exile (586 B.C.). The Palestinian state of Yahweh worshipers, restored by the Persians in 538 B.C., I will call *Judea,* and the worshipers of Yahweh, both in the re-established state and scattered about the ancient world, I shall call *the Jews.*

ninth century it lost much of its territory in an ill-advised revolt against the Assyrians, who had reduced it also to a tribute-paying satellite. It remained for a new-old power to deliver the final blow. Babylonia rallied the forces of the southern plain of Mesopotamia and, in alliance with the Medes of the Iranian plateau, overthrew Assyria and seized its empire. With remarkable fatuousness, the last kings of Judah clung to an alliance with the crumbling power of Egypt against the neo-Babylonian Empire and consequently suffered the fate of the northern kingdom of Ephraim. Nebuchadnezzar conquered Judah, besieged and utterly destroyed Jerusalem, the religious and political center of the little state, in 586, and sent most of the richer inhabitants of the land into exile in Babylonia.

THE SURVIVAL OF ISRAEL

Here should have ended the history of the people of Israel, for they had suffered the ultimate disaster. Having carved out a homeland and rooted themselves and their hopes and aspirations in its soil, they were cut away from their roots by the Babylonian conquest and became exiles in a strange land. For a dozen other peoples who underwent a similar experience, the catastrophe proved fatal; they gradually merged or sank into the civilization in the midst of which they were resettled and lost their identity as peoples. Socially, economically, and politically the people of Israel differed little from the swarm of petty states of the Fertile Crescent that vanished from the pages of history between the tenth and the fifth centuries B.C., obliterated forever by conquering Assyrians, neo-Babylonians, and Persians.

By all rules and precedents, then, the people of Israel should have vanished, too—but they did not. They survive to our own day; they are now called Jews, and in this very day they have again survived a disaster of unprecedented magnitude—the Nazi campaign of extermination. They not only survived the catastrophe of the sixth century B.C., they also fathered two world religions. The prophet Mohammed, founder of Islam, looked to the religion of the Jews for inspiration. And Jesus, the founder of Christianity, was himself a Jew whose attachment to the faith of his fathers made the holy books of the Jews a part of the Christian revelation—the Old Testament.

The survival of a people for hundreds of years without a land for them to be the people of seems incongruous and in a way unnatural. It seems at least to require an explanation. The Jews of the fifth century B.C. would have readily agreed that their survival was quite unnatural and, indeed, required an explanation. They were sure they knew what that explanation was: *their god had saved them from the destruction he visited on all their neighbors.* Whether in the final analysis it was indeed Yahweh,[2] the god of the Jews, who saved his people from destruction, the historian will never be able to say. What he can say with very considerable assurance is that what the Jews believed about their god prevented them from vanishing, as all their neighbors did, when they lost their homeland. It was their religion alone that saved the Jews, their religion that distinguished them from their neighbors, their religion that warrants the relatively detailed consideration that we have already given to the Israelites, an otherwise quite unspectacular people of the ancient Near East.

2. The name of the god of Israel is spelled Jehovah in the King James and the Douai versions of the Bible. Present-day scholars generally agree that the proper translation from Hebrew is Yahweh.

THE RELIGION OF ISRAEL

The Source Book

Our principal source of information about the history of Israel's idea of its god and of its relation to him is a bulky anthology of Hebrew literature. Except for this anthology our historical evidence on the religion of Israel before the Exile in Babylon is slight—a few statements in the documents of peoples who had contact with the Hebrews, a considerable mass of archaeological finds, and some inferences drawn from the religious practices of modern Semitic nomads and of the contemporaries of the Israelites.

This anthology, which forms the Old Testament of the Christian Bible, is remarkably full. We have already said something about it in our story of Israel's notions about its own secular history. The writings collected in it, however, so profoundly affected the history of the Jews, and subsequently the history of the Christians, and thereby the history of the Western world, that we must look at the Old Testament more closely.

The Old Testament contains selections that cover a period of about a thousand years and a very wide range of literary genres. There are collections of hymns, or Psalms, and of ancient wise adages, or Proverbs. There are folk tales like the Samson story, and literary romances such as the Books of Ruth and Esther. There is a great passionate religious dialogue, the Book of Job, and a witty essay by a world-weary skeptic, Ecclesiastes. There is a collection of love lyrics, the Song of Solomon.

Despite the literary grandeur of these writings, and of others incorporated into the Old Testament, the purpose of the men who over the centuries put the anthology together was not primarily aesthetic—to please; it was didactic—to teach. The writings preserved and transmitted in the holy book were for the instruction of the Jews, "the remnant of Israel," who survived the Babylonian captivity. Some of this remnant returned to Palestine after 538 B.C. under the protection of the Persian conquerors of the neo-Babylonian Empire; others remained scattered throughout the Persian Empire and the Hellenistic states which, after Alexander's conquests, held fragments of that dismembered empire in the Near East. The collection of holy writings was intended to teach the Jews about Israel's god, Yahweh, and the terms of the Jews' covenant with him.

Although occasionally new books—among them probably Job and Ecclesiastes, and certainly Esther and Daniel—found a permanent place in the Bible, the very core of the anthology was made up of works which had been set down before the fall of the Babylonian conquerors of Judah. These works constituted the laws which governed worship of Yahweh and the conduct of life of his worshipers with respect to each other and to the non-Jewish populations with which Jews necessarily came into contact. The law properly so called (Torah) was contained in the first five books (Pentateuch) of the anthology. Here the original dealing of Yahweh with his chosen people from the beginning of the world to their entrance into Canaan is set forth and commented on. In addition, the historical works record the actual attempts of the Jews to improvise institutions for the proper observance of the law in particular situations in which they found themselves. There are also the utterances of certain men who claimed to speak for Israel's god as a consequence of special religious insights granted them by that god—the Prophets. All of these works return again and again to a single theme, however: the need and the duty of the people of Israel, whether as individuals or as a nation, to obey in thought and deed the will of Israel's god, and the consequences of their success or failure to do so. It is this collection that, with a few modifications, became the Old Testament of the Christian Bible, the Holy Writ of the Jews.

It might seem that such an anthology would be an ideal source of information about the history of Israel's idea of its god. However, what the men who compiled the anthology present to us as history varies enormously in historical value. At one extreme there is the most accurate and forthright kind of narrative, written near the time of the events described. Such, for example, is the history of the reigns of Saul and David. At the other extreme is the most obvious sort of legend such as the genealogies of the families who inhabited the earth from the time of Adam to Noah, families whose patriarchs lived, the book says, about eight hundred years apiece. Soon we realize that our compilers of the history of the Israelites and their god were not mere historians, primarily concerned to report a story about certain events in exact conformity to the available evidence. They were men with a theory of history. They not only reported and reproduced the ancient tales and written documents of their people; they edited and they retouched and they interpreted them, all in accordance with their theory of history, that is, in accordance with their notion of the significance of the events in throwing light on the right relation of the children of Israel to Yahweh. We have already spoken of the arduous efforts of scholars during the past century to sift the actual facts about the early history of the Israelites out of the matrix of myth and legend in which they are embedded. As a result of these learned labors many obscure points have been cleared up and the basic shape of Israel's religious development has emerged. On the other hand much remains, and will perhaps always remain, uncertain.

The Teachers of Israel

What the beliefs of the tribes of Israel were in the misty beginnings of their history we cannot know. The early history of those pastoral wanderers was long preserved only in oral tradition. The old tales passed from father to son, generation after generation. By the time they got set down in writing, centuries had elapsed. By the time that any of the *surviving* accounts were written, the people of Israel had had several tremendous and well-remembered experiences. The earliest writers, setting down stories already old in their day, sometimes read into the tales of the patriarchs meanings related to Israel's later experiences—religious meanings that the simple shepherds who were the heroes of the stories might have had some difficulty in understanding. Experts on these matters have been unable to agree how much of the record that we now have is good oral tradition and how much is later revision.

One thing, however, is certain. The Israelite tribes had been wandering about the inner fringe of the Fertile Crescent for centuries before they received their religion and became followers of the god with whom thereafter their destinies were forever linked. Even here there are difficulties. For although it is clear that some Israelites did become the people of Yahweh at an ascertainable moment, it is not at all clear what this event meant to the Israelites at that time, what they had in mind when they pledged themselves henceforth to be the people of Yahweh. Both probability and the later history of the Israelites indicate that at the time they did not all have the same thing in mind. Many Israelites likely had very little in mind at all, then or later; the history of the people is marked by the stolid resistance of this ordinary mass to the inspired but rather demanding teachers who insisted that the Israelites' god required them to act in ways spectacularly different from the ways of their neighbors in the melting pot that was Canaan.

It was the profound religious experiences, magnificent moral fervor, and inexhaustible zeal of Israel's leaders, from Moses, who took charge of the flight from Egypt, to the prophets of the Babylonian exile, that ultimately triumphed over the easy ways of the Israelite people and even over the shortcomings of the leaders themselves. Thus as the story of Israel that matters historically is the story of Israel's religion, so that part of the story of Israel's religion that matters historically is the story of Israel's religious geniuses.

Yahweh and Israel

The religion of the Jews who returned to Judea from their exile in Babylon in the sixth century B.C. bears the marks of three great episodes in the religious tradition of Israel: (1) the covenant of Yahweh with the people of Israel, (2) the working out of a distinctive body of law for that people, and (3) the prophetic movement. The prophetic movement falls into three periods: that of the eighth-century prophets, who came to the fore during the Assyrian peril, that of the seventh-century prophets, who warned Judah of the coming disaster, the total destruction of the Judaic state by its enemies, and that of the prophets of the Exile, who upheld the hopes of the Jews in the bitterness of the Babylonian captivity after the fall of Jerusalem in 586 B.C.

The Covenant   The great event for the people of Israel—the one that in their view lay at the very foundation of the nation—was the exodus from bondage in Egypt. According to tradition, however, the flight from the Egyptians was not merely political, it was also religious. It was during their wanderings in the wilderness after the exodus that the Israelites came to know their god Yahweh and through the liberator-prophet Moses entered into a covenant or solemn agreement with him. The people of Israel believed that Yahweh had not only led them out of the land of Egypt but agreed to make of them "a peculiar treasure . . . above all people . . . a kingdom of priests and a holy nation" (Exodus 19:5, 6). In return the Israelites promised to obey the god who had saved them and chosen them for his very own. To obey him was to obey his law. It was during their wanderings in the wastelands after the flight from Egypt that the Israelites received from Moses the first edition of Yahweh's law, the Ten Commandments. Of these commandments the first was that, as a people, the children of Israel should worship no other god but Yahweh: "Thou shalt have no other gods before me."

Thus it was—so the men who wrote down and edited the Old Testament believed—that Israel conquered the Promised Land, Canaan, which their god had given over to them, in the name of that national god, Yahweh. As Israel extended its dominion in Canaan, more and more Israelites settled down to enjoy the benefits of Yahweh's favor. They turned from a seminomadic existence to the way of life of the farmer and city-dweller. In the process they were drawn into even closer contact with the Canaanites, and the relatively backward Israelites naturally tended to assimilate the culture of the more advanced ancient inhabitants.

This was bound to cause difficulty in the matter of religion. The Canaanites had stood for centuries along the line of march of the great ancient empires and had absorbed the nature-gods of many oriental cults into their local religion. Their gods were deeply involved in the great natural forces on which farmers depended. They were divine agricultural specialists, skilled in meeting the wants of an agricultural people. As the Israelites were being gradually transformed from pastoral tribes into a settled urban-farming people, they experienced a division of allegiance between Yahweh on one side and the old nature-gods of Canaan on the other. A considerable difference of opinion arose among them as to how far they had committed themselves when they became Yahweh's people. To many of the farming settlers, dependent on very capricious natural forces for their bread, it seemed imprudent and perhaps even impious not to rally all the supernatural farming help they could, including whatever help the old gods of Canaan might have to offer. Other Israelites felt that their brethren who offered sacrifices to the numerous Baals or gods of Canaan were up to no good, worshiping idols, an activity of which Yahweh was notoriously jealous. Yet despite their differences of opinion about the precise relationship of Yahweh to the gods of Canaan, on one point the Israelites were agreed: *Yahweh alone was the god of all Israel, Israel alone was his chosen people.*

The Law of Israel   As the tribes of pastoral wanderers settled into Canaan their way of life changed, and as men's lives change so must their law change. The law of Israel settled in Canaan had three main sources: the customs of the shepherd ancestors of the Israelites, the customs of the land they came to live in, and the laws transmitted by Moses to Israel. With local variations, the law of Canaan seems to have been a body of rules and practices generally applied among the settled people of the Fertile Crescent all the way around from the lower Mesopotamian plain to

Canaan. Allowing for some regional variation, this law has much in common with the Akkadian-Sumerian custom codified in the eighteenth century B.C. by Hammurabi. The precise content of Mosaic law can no longer be determined with certainty, but it probably included the religious and moral rules of the Ten Commandments and some laws about the form of worship demanded by Yahweh. The ingredients drawn from the three sources were blended, elaborated, and extended as time went on to form the common law of the people of Israel. Thus a bond of law, as well as the common historical tradition of the Covenant, bound together a people who were divided politically before the time of Saul and after the death of Solomon.

In their discussions of the components of ancient Hebrew law, specialists sometimes distinguish between those elements in it which make specific demands upon the faithful (such as the requirement of a money payment for an offense given to a neighbor) and those which, as in the Ten Commandments, specifically prohibit certain kinds of moral behavior (such as "Thou shalt not kill"). While not always the case, it is generally thought that the former kind of legislation was borrowed by the Jews from the peoples among whom they had settled, at one time or another, in the ancient Near East, or derived from their earlier tribal period as a part of the common heritage of tribal peoples in that area. The latter kind of legislation, called *apodictic* laws, reflects the uniquely Hebrew contribution to world ethical teachings. Whereas the former kind of law is too specific to be followed precisely or to be modified in response to the historical situation in which an individual Israelite might find himself, the latter kind ("Thou shalt not . . .") establishes the general nature of the moral requirements laid upon the Israelite by his god. Of course, the letter of the apodictic legislation could not always be followed in every situation either, and this is why the great teachers of Israel turned their attention continually to its interpretation in relation to specific historical situations. Since the Jews believed that this legislation descended directly from God to Moses and expressed precisely what God wanted of His people, there could be no doubting its imperative character. But since they also believed that God was just and would presumably not lay an injunction upon His people which they could not fulfill, the teachers and prophets were increasingly to interpret the "spirit" of the injunction as against the "letter," thereby "spiritualizing" their conception of God and of themselves.

The Prophets　At many times and in many lands men or women have undergone a sudden emotional upheaval in which they believed themselves the recipients of a special revelation from a divine source. Such states are called ecstatic. The prophets of Israel were ecstatics. They were called prophets because they declared (*pro-phimi*) the will of the deity, not only for the present, but as it had been in the past and would be in the future as well. Prophecy was a profession among the Israelites. Almost every king kept his seers, who provided him with prognostications that guided his policies. Some of these were prophets of the various Canaanite gods, whose worship some of the kings of Ephraim and Judah permitted and, on occasion, even promoted. But the prophets who ultimately triumphed in the religious life of the Israelites were those who claimed to be prophets of Yahweh alone.

Among these prophets of Yahweh there emerged in the ninth century a group characterized by their opposition to what they regarded as unholy practices among the Israelites. The greatest of these "opposition prophets" was Elijah. Elijah and his follower

Elisha were shocked by the growing tendency of the children of Israel, and especially of the kings, to divide their religious favors between Yahweh and a great many other gods and goddesses. They regarded the rites and services rendered to the gods of the land, the native fertility deities of Canaan, as a breach of Israel's covenant and an outrageous affront to Yahweh. They predicted awful divine retaliations against rulers who, as they said, "went whoring after other gods." On the face of it these early opposition prophets were a failure. The kings of the Israelites and their subjects went right on setting a great variety of gods beside Yahweh, if not before him. But at a time when the Israelites were taking more and more to the ways of their neighbors, Elijah and his followers kept vivid the remembrance of Israel's first allegiance—their covenant with Yahweh.

It was on the foundation laid by the opposition prophets that the so-called "writing prophets" built their great work in the two hundred years that began in the middle of the eighth century, so disastrous materially and so profitable spiritually for Israel. It was the writing prophets alone who prepared Israel for the dreadful political disasters of the age—an era when wave after wave of Assyrians, Egyptians, and Babylonians swept across the lands of the Israelites, destroying towns, slaughtering the conquered, making a monstrous joke of all Israel's pretensions to earthly power. When the ultimate disaster came—the fall of Jerusalem, the destruction of Yahweh's great temple there, and the resettlement of a vast number of the people themselves in the Mesopotamian valley—it was again the prophets who saved the uprooted nation from perishing, restored its hope, and renewed its dreams of a glorious future for the chosen people of God.

The writing prophets are so called because their words were preserved in writing, sometimes, apparently, almost as they were uttered. While the politicians and paid prophets foretold fat times and victory for Israel, the great free prophets went among the people of the Israelite cities, prophesying misery and woe. The first of these outriders of the coming disaster, Amos, exhibited from the outset the full power of the prophetic message. He went through the list of Israel's neighbors—Damascus, the cities of Philistia, the Phoenician city of Tyre, and the people to Israel's east and south, Ammonites, Moabites, Edomites—all these, said Amos, God would soon utterly destroy because of their violence and barbarity in war. And note, He would destroy some of them not for their violence to Israel but for their violence to *one another*. Yahweh, Amos said, was not merely the god of Israel, concerned with its narrow affairs; He was the Lord of all nations, and He punished the iniquity of all nations.[3] And what of His own people of Judah and Ephraim? The people of Judah "have not kept His commandments, and their lies caused them to err"; the people of Ephraim "sold the righteous for silver and the poor for a pair of shoes." "Therefore," said the God of Israel, "I will send fire upon Judah, and it shall devour the palaces of Jerusalem." For Ephraim the time was coming when "flight shall fail the swift . . . neither shall the mighty save himself . . . and he that is courageous among the mighty shall flee away naked." And for all of Israel: "I will cause you to go into captivity beyond Damascus." As to the great day of Yahweh,

---

3. The place at which we ought to stop speaking of Yahweh, the national god of Israel, and speak of God, the Maker and Ruler of all, is hard to settle on, since the children of Israel themselves took a long time to make up their minds individually and collectively on this point. By shifting from lower case to capitals in the initial letter of "God" and by gradually dropping the name Yahweh I have tried to suggest this transition typographically.

when the Israelites expected their God to establish His chosen people in power: "Woe unto you that desire the day of the Lord . . . the day of the Lord is darkness and not light . . . even very dark, and no brightness in it."

This was indeed a strange teaching. Yahweh would destroy His own people, uproot them, take from them the land He had given them, the very holy places where they worshiped Him. How and why should such a thing be? "Ah, children of Israel . . . which I brought up from the land of Egypt . . . you only have I known of all the families of the earth: *therefore I will punish you for all your iniquities.*"*

This was the kernel of the message of the great prophets. The sins of all peoples would be visited on them by God. But on Israel, His own people with whom He had entered into a special pact and to whom He had revealed the law of righteousness, His wrath would fall most hard; for, knowing the good way through God's very words, they had yet followed the evil way. So they would fall to a conqueror and eat the bitter bread of exile in a strange land.

The thing foreseen by the prophets came to pass, first to Ephraim and then to Judah. But even before the final catastrophe and increasingly after it, the prophets struck a new note, a note of hope amid the general misery of a beaten people. Their prophecy of doom had steeled the spirit of Israel to meet disaster and above all not to see in it the total defeat of their god Yahweh by gods of the Assyrians and the Babylonians. Rather, they saw in their own desolation a proof of the vast power of their Lord,

---

*Italics here and following pages are the author's and are used for emphasis.

whose glory and majesty were such that He had no need of a piece of land or of the altars Israel built Him on that land or of the sacrifices and burnt offerings rendered Him on these altars. But once they endured the terrible wrench of exile, the scattered Israelites needed something to brace their courage lest, fearing that their God had forever forsaken them, they fall into despair or seek hope and consolation by rendering service to the gods of the lands where they lived. The later prophets, therefore, more and more stressed God's loving kindness, His enduring tenderness toward the people He had chosen above all others, and His readiness to forgive an Israel, terribly punished, that would turn to Him with contrite heart, repent its wickedness, and walk thereafter in the way of righteousness according to His commandments. During those days of Yahweh, of which Amos had spoken, that were darkness and not light, the fragmented community was sustained by words of comfort that the prophets had spoken. God would not forsake His child, Israel. Thus, movingly, the great poet-prophet of the exile spoke of God's forgiveness and His coming re-establishment of Israel:

Comfort ye, comfort ye, my people, saith your God. Speak ye comfortably to Jerusalem, and cry unto her, that her warfare is accomplished, that her iniquity is pardoned, for she hath received of the Lord's hand double for all her sins.

Thou art my servant, O Israel, thou shalt not be forgotten of me. I have blotted out as a thick cloud thy transgressions, and as a cloud thy sins: return unto Me, for I have redeemed thee. Sing, O ye heavens: . . . break forth into singing, ye mountains . . . for the Lord hath redeemed Jacob and glorified Himself in Israel.

THE GOD OF THE JEWS

When, as the prophets had presumably foreseen, "the remnant of Israel" returned from exile to an impoverished and shrunken Judea, they came back with a religion, a vision of God and His relation to man, that had been wrought out and tried in the fire of seven centuries of history. That vision was to undergo some modifications in the future, but its primary features suffered no further basic change at the hands of the Jews, the direct heirs of Israel. It also became an essential part of Christianity, and thus it underlies the religion of the whole of the Western world today.

The Jews' conception of God and their contribution to man's religious experience have been described as ethical monotheism: belief in the unity and goodness of the divine. In its chilly abstractness, however, this term does poor justice to the Jewish vision of God, which was always warm, vivid, and concrete. For the Jews there was but one God, Yahweh.

. . . *Who created the world and all that was in it:*

"The Lord . . . created the heavens and stretched them out; He . . . spread forth the earth and that which cometh out of it; He . . . giveth breath unto the people upon it, and spirit to them that walk therein." The gods of other peoples, the gods to whom even Israel at times had offered sacrifices, were mere idols, man-made pieces of wood, powerless, fit for making a fire but not to worship, for shall a man "fall down to the stock of a tree?"

. . . *Who ruled the world:*

The God who created the world did not then abdicate and turn it over to others to rule. He ruled it Himself, sometimes through agents who knew Him not. The Assyrians, who crushed

Ephraim, the Babylonians, who destroyed the Assyrians and desolated Judah, the Persians, who destroyed Babylon and restored Judah—all these were but servants of Yahweh, servants who unwittingly executed His will, knowing neither Him nor His will.

. . . Who chose Israel as His People:

Only Israel knew Him and His will, for only to Israel had He revealed Himself. He revealed Himself when He saved the children of Israel from Pharaoh, chose them to be His own people, made a covenant with them to be their God, and through Moses gave them His commandments. He continued to reveal Himself in the working out of His law, in the words He spoke through the voices of the prophets, in the destinies of peoples, and especially in the destiny of the Chosen People.

. . . Who was a jealous God:

Through all His revelations the Jews knew that Yahweh was a jealous God who demanded that His people worship Him and Him alone, a wrathful God who had already visited terrible punishments on His people for their defection from their covenant with Him to worship and obey Him.

. . . Who was a righteous God:

This jealous God, who would have His people worship none but Him, was not satisfied with mere worship, however. Sacrifice at the altar, offerings, formal prayers were not enough, from evil men they were nothing:

"Though ye offer Me burnt offerings . . . I will not accept them. . . . When ye spread forth your hands, I will hide Mine eyes from you. . . . *Your hands are full of blood.*"

Yahweh rejected the prayers of oppressors who came before Him with blood on their hands because He was a righteous God, and He demanded righteousness of all men. Especially He demanded it of Israel, to whom alone He had directly spoken His will:

"Cease to do evil, learn to do well, seek judgment, relieve the oppressed, judge the fatherless, plead for the widow. . . . What doth the Lord require of thee but to do justly, and to love mercy, and to walk humbly with thy God."

. . . Who was just and punished iniquity:

His will was that men do right and refrain from doing wrong; if men who knew His will disobeyed it, if Israel sinned, then Israel must be punished, for the wrathful righteous God was a *just* God and turned His anger against injustice:

"Woe unto them that call evil good and good evil, that put darkness for light and light for darkness . . . Woe unto them . . . which justify the wicked for reward and take away the righteousness of the righteous from Him. . . . They have sown the wind and they shall reap the whirlwind."

. . . Who was a perfect law giver:

The sin of Israel against Yahweh was the worst because He had made His will so clear. It was embodied in the *Torah,* the law. If they had followed that law, the Chosen People would not have gone wrong, for Yahweh was the perfect law giver:

"The *law* of the Lord is perfect converting the soul; the testimony of the Lord is sure making wise the simple. The *statutes* of the Lord are right rejoicing the heart: the *commandment* of the Lord is pure enlightening the heart."

. . . Who was a loving God:

The God of Israel was a God of justice, so His people must suffer for their sins—their deeds of injustice and their worship of other gods. But He was also a God of love, a loving father, who sorrowed for the affliction of His children:

"Whom the Lord loveth He chastiseth; even as a father the son in whom he delighteth."

Thus the love of Yahweh for Israel did not die with their disobedience; it was eternal: "I have loved thee with an everlasting love."

. . . Who was a merciful God:

The Jewish God of wrath and justice and love is also a forgiving God, a God of *mercy.* Let Israel but repent and Yahweh will end the sufferings of His children; the Scourge of Israel will become the Redeemer of Israel:

"They shall come with weeping and supplications and I will lead them; I will cause them to walk by the rivers of waters in a straight way; wherein they shall not stumble, for I am a father to Israel."

"In a little wrath I hid my face from thee for a moment; but with everlasting kindness will I have mercy on thee, saith the Lord, thy Redeemer."

. . . Who, through Israel, will save all men:

Israel indeed must be redeemed, for it had a great destiny. In the end all nations would turn to Israel, realizing that Israel's God was the only God; and then all men would worship the one true God together:

"The word is gone out of my mouth in righteousness and shall not return, that unto me *every* knee shall bend, *every* tongue shall swear."

"And many nations shall come and say, come, let us go up to . . . the house of the God of Jacob, and He will teach us His ways, and we will walk in His paths. . . . And He shall judge among many people and rebuke strong nations afar off, and they shall beat their swords into plowshares and their spears into pruning hooks; nation shall not lift up a sword against nation, neither shall they learn war any more. But they shall sit every man under his vine and under his fig tree; and none shall make them afraid, for the mouth of the Lord of hosts hath spoken it."

Thus the Jewish vision of Yahweh ended in the dream of a just and righteous world, where all people recognized Israel's God as their own, and worshiped Him, and obeyed His law, and lived in peace together. In that day the Lord Yahweh would establish the Kingdom of God on earth and He would reign over all mankind, for all mankind would have become Israel.

THE JEWS AND THE "WORLD"

Scholars who have painstakingly studied the history and religion of the ancient Jews have found embedded in them bits of beliefs and practices picked up from many other peoples. For the Israelites had had much contact with other peoples in the long centuries from before their first entry into south Syria to the time when the remnant returned to Judea after the captivity in Babylon. But the more scholars have studied the matter, the more certain they have become that the "borrowings" of Israel from its neighbors were not essential, that whatever the Jews took they transformed, and that at its very foundation the religion of Israel was unique. In their conception of God and man's relation to Him the Jews had made a radically new departure of such historical force that today in the Western world, twenty-five centuries later, that conception plays a major part in guiding men's thought and actions and shaping their destinies. I shall single out a few traits of the religion of the ancient Jews to show how they differed from all their neighbors and to suggest how that religion, through Christianity, has exercised an enduring or a recurrent influence on the Western world.

The Minimizing of Magic

Magic stands at the very threshold of history. Among the earliest records we have of civilized man we find evidence that he practiced magic, and it is also general among primitive peoples today. Moreover, magic is not just a sign of "backwardness." It has persisted among several of the most highly developed civilizations—the Chinese, the Indian, the Egyptian, the Mesopotamian. Therefore, it is neither an accident, nor is it particularly primitive. It is a means by which many peoples have sought to deal with unknown and presumably supernatural agents of human evil and suffering. Evil and suffering, a part of the experience of every man who has ever lived, have seemed to indicate to most peoples that there is in the world, imbedded in the very nature of things, a streak of hostility to man and his purposes. This streak of hostility men sometimes ascribed to the gods, whom they envisaged as indifferent to man's welfare, or as annoyed with him, or, in some respects, as his enemy. Or they ascribed the hostility to malignant spirits, beings existing somewhere in the twilight world between man and the gods, who have it in for mankind. In either case, the warding off of evil became an important part of the business of life. The strategy of defense against hostile supernatural forces was to find a particu-

lar rite or object or formula that would fend off, appease, or fool
the dangerous divinity or demon, or would summon to the aid of
the victim a friendly god or spirit. Given the endless array of
human misfortunes, men's natural desire to avoid them, and the
large number of possible malignant agents in polytheistic religions, the practice of magic was sure to be a very complicated
affair, a business for experts. It was also likely to be a business
that paid rather well.

From its beginning in the Covenant, the religion of Israel left
little room for magic, and its subsequent development only
diminished that small latitude. The Jews did not have to wonder
where—out of what divine or devilish source—suffering and evil
came from. Directly or indirectly it came, like all else, from God
Himself: "I form the light and create darkness: I make peace *and
create evil:* I the Lord do all these things." Suffering was God's just
punishment of men for their own wickedness, and He was not
one to be put off from His purpose by a magician's tricks of
trade. Indeed, in relation to such a God, coercive magic could
only be impious. It was also unnecessary, for God had given
Israel the remedy for suffering: to turn from evil and repent; to
obey God's law. That law was no mystery. In old Israel it was
used daily to settle disputes. Before the Exile a number of written collections of it seem to have circulated. After the end of the
Exile it was incorporated into books.

The Book and the Law

Gradually the books of the Law and other writing wherein God
was supposed to have revealed Himself were incorporated into
one great book—the sacred scripture of the Jews. Thenceforth
the Jews became the people of a book. Since there was nothing
secret about what was in the Book, the priests were never able to

sustain the pretensions of priests in many other lands: they could not claim to have special knowledge of what their God was up to and what He wanted; they could not pretend to be specially authorized agents of their God's will except in the performance of rituals. Any Jew who could read Hebrew could find out God's will. In this sense at least the Jews became "a kingdom of priests and a holy nation," and among many Jews the authority of students of the Book, who could interpret God's will, stood far higher than the authority of the priests, who performed the sacrifices before His altar in the Temple at Jerusalem.

Substantially, God's will was simple: it was, as I have said, that the Jews keep the Covenant of their forefathers with Him and obey His law. Much of God's law for the Jews was concerned with right conduct in society. It was no more elevated in its standards than the laws of neighboring people. Some of the law concerned worship; it laid down rules for ritual cleanness, prescribed the foods that God's worshiper might eat, set forth the holy days he must celebrate. The first rule of all was that *the Jews must worship only Yahweh and only in the way He commanded.* It was this revealed command of their jealous God that distinguished the ancient Jews from the ancient *gentiles,* which simply means ordinary peoples as against the Chosen People.

The Religion of One God

Several times in several places in the ancient world, speculative thinkers came to the conclusion that behind all appearances of a multiplicity of mysterious superhuman forces there was only one divine being. Thus these thinkers achieved a *philosophy of monotheism.* This one divine being that men thought their way to did not unmistakably command anything; He made no special revelation of His will, if indeed so abstract a being might be said to have a will. Therefore intellectual monotheists went right on making the customary religious offerings to the many gods whom their fellow countrymen worshiped and believed in, regarding each divinity as a different manifestation of the single divine being. Because they continued to act precisely as their fellow countrymen acted with respect to the gods, their monotheism did not in the least interfere with the prevailing polytheism, which retained its hold among ordinary people. In fact no ancient people en masse attained a religion of one god except the Jews. The firm foundation of the religion of the Jews was not a matter of speculative opinion about "the unity of the divine," a divine something that did nothing and said nothing. The religion of the Jews was the religion of one God, a very personal God who both spoke and acted with a great deal of vigor, who revealed Himself and, according to the teaching which ultimately won general acceptance among His followers, absolutely commanded that the Jews worship none but Him, and that they worship Him exactly as He prescribed. Thus Jewish monotheism did not merely float rootless in the minds of intellectuals, it had firm roots in the *monolatry* of the Jews—the service they gave to their jealous God alone.

The Separateness of the Jews

When the Persians ended their captivity, by no means all the families that had gone into exile after the Babylonian conquest returned to Judea. Many Jews remained scattered all over the ancient world and multiplied wondrously. For the peoples amid whom they settled, these dispersed Jews posed a peculiar problem. For the Egyptians, the Babylonians, and all other ancient peoples religious and political life were intermixed. The gods of the city or the land were its protectors and lords. If a man lived in a place, he was naturally expected to obey its laws and render its rulers what was due them. Just as naturally he was expected to render its divine protectors their due, to take his part in the religious rites of the community. This was precisely what the Jew could not do. He could worship and obey his God and no other god. Not only could he not worship with his fellow-citizens, he could not mingle with them socially in the most ordinary of ways. The law of the God of Israel also established dietary regulations that made it impossible for a Jew to eat in his gentile neighbor's house without risking a breach of God's law, that is, without falling into sin. Thus the Jews might reside long among another people yet always remain apart from them, living as strangers in the land where they were born. They thus embodied in practice a new idea, an idea that was to have a long and troubled future. For they lived as if the demands of religion transcended—were different from and above—the current laws of any particular society. In case of a conflict between the law of his God and the law of the community he lived in, the Jew was bound to obey his God. Never before had the issue between the obedience due to God and the obedience due to man been clearly raised; never thereafter was it wholly to disappear, even to our own day.

GOD, NATURE, AND HISTORY

The people of the Western world take the importance of history for granted. They simply assume that things have changed from what they once were, that it is worthwhile to know something of the way things used to be, and that this knowledge of a past different from the present in some sense illuminates the present. It is therefore difficult for us to realize that many great civilizations have been wholly indifferent to, indeed virtually incapable of imagining in a significantly sophisticated way, their own past as something distinct from their present existence. The stream of events flowing from the past to the present seemed so unimportant to such peoples that they simply did not bother to record much about it.

In fact, the first people to feel deeply about their own past in a specifically historical sense, and therefore the first people to produce real historians, were the people of Israel. The Mesopotamians may have faintly glimpsed the idea of the coherence of happenings in time; the Egyptians seem to have had no notion of it at all. Both had a tradition of stories about a time when chaos ruled the world and myths that accounted for the emergence of an ordered sphere of human activity through the agency of the gods, but both seemed also to have believed that once the primeval disposition had been made no fundamental changes could be wrought in the resulting world order, either by gods or men. Both peoples also imagined an afterlife which was a reward for men who had fulfilled their obligations to the world order created by the gods out of chaos. But neither regarded the temporal process as a series of individual events constituting a coherent sequence of change.

Since they believed their rulers to be gods or representatives of gods, they assumed that their rulers' actions were perfectly consonant with the actions of the gods performed at the time of the creation. That the rulers might deviate from the divine pattern was unthinkable, and if such deviations appeared to take place to the reflective observer, it was assumed that the observer himself had failed to see the continuity underlying the change, not that things had really undergone a fundamental alteration. In short, the world as it appeared to the ancient Egyptian and

Mesopotamian was a fixed and changeless continuum wherein men were born, lived out their lives in a manner as closely approximating that of their fathers as possible, and died. The important thing was to adjust one's actions to the changeless order of the cosmos as reflected in the regular movements of the stars, the sun, the rivers, and the seasons. As the writer of Ecclesiastes, who seems to have been influenced by such ideas, puts it:

> The sun also riseth, and the sun goeth down, and hasteth to his place where he rose. The wind goeth toward the south, and turneth about unto the north . . . the wind returneth again. . . . All the rivers turn into the sea; yet the sea is not full; unto the place from whence the rivers come, thither they return again. One generation passeth away and another generation cometh, but the earth abideth forever. The thing that hath been, it is that which shall be, and that which is done is that which shall be done: *and there is no new thing under the sun.*

Variation, change, development were representative of the disorder against which the gods had fought and won in the earliest beginnings of the world. To have taken delight or interest in this disorder would not only have been foolish, it would have been an act of gross impiety.

Therefore, ancient Mesopotamian and Egyptian chronicles always stress the similarity of things in the present to things as they were before. The various Egyptian kings can be distinguished as individual personalities only with the greatest difficulty because it was the purpose of the ancient chroniclers to demonstrate the specific king's divinity by showing the similarities between his actions and those of other kings known to memory. To have admitted a defeat of a king in battle would have been to cast doubt on the king's divinity. Similarly, to give credit for a notable achievement to someone other than the king would have been to accord to a mere human the power which resided in the king alone. This is why the history of Egypt and Meso-potamia as we read it today is a history *reconstructed by* modern scholars from documents that had no historical end in view when they were written—myths, folk tales, laws, temple and business records, burial inscriptions, treatises on medicine, and magical formularies.

By contrast, today the history of ancient Israel is *written* on the basis of history *written by* Israelites 2,500 to 3,000 years ago and contained in the Bible. The whole framework of that book is historical in intention. This is not to say, of course, that the historical vision of the Israelites can be separated from their religious conceptions. But since the religion of the Israelites differed so markedly from that of other peoples in the ancient Near East, their conception of history differed also. It would not be too strong to say that the religion of Israel differed from the rest precisely in the degree to which, having distinguished their God from physical nature, they also were forced to conceive of a special *historical* sphere within which the drama between a super-natural god and a specifically human nature could unfold.

The other peoples of the ancient Near East, because their religious energies were poured out on gods imbedded in or identified with natural objects and processes, turned their face to nature and their back to history. But the Israelites could not do this. The big thing for them was not a myth about the constancy and fruitfulness of nature but about a supernatural deity who turned both natural and human events to His own higher, moral purpose. The Exodus from Egypt, the Covenant with God, and the reception of His law were not natural, recurring events, but unique events in the life of a unique people, hence *historical* events.

The nature of the Covenant made the Israelites, as a group and individually, partners in the working out of God's will in time. In a sense, the history of Israel was a prolonged dialogue with its God, one in which God acted, and acted mightily, that His will be done, but also one in which men acted in the full knowledge of what God required of them and in full freedom to cooperate with God (and prosper) or defy Him (and suffer disaster). The transcendentalism of the Israelites allowed them to distinguish their God from nature; their conception of the importance of the Covenant allowed them to distinguish man from both nature and God. Nature could be regarded by the Israelites as a stage upon which an essentially moral drama unfolded, on which two actors—with unequal dignity to be sure, God on the one hand, man on the other—played their respective parts. The lesson to be learned from history, the ancient Israelites believed, was a moral lesson; the principles which governed history could be known. But they vested responsibility for disaster in man who, knowing from the law what God desired of him, presumed to follow his own course. Thus, by a curious paradox, the acts of both good men and evil men were worth saving to consciousness, for both showed equally the justice, mercy, and power of God. To be sure, what modern historians would regard as economic and political events per se were not distinguished from moral or religious events by the ancient Hebrew chroniclers; in the end, they believed, every political success and every economic success was a result of God's will, not of man's power. But this interest in the operations of the moral law in the determination of individual destinies promoted an acute psychological sense and a sharp feeling for detail which have been characteristic elements of great historical analysis ever since the unknown writer of the drama of Saul undertook to sketch the story of the perils of kingly power. So it was with those who sought to portray the events in the remote past which had resulted in God's choice of Israel as the object of His special concern.

The very birth of Israel was wrapped in history, and Israel never forgot it. At all times its great religious leaders took their inspiration from these first events in Israel's history. In the days of settlement in Canaan when so many Israelites were doing the "natural" thing and taking up the worship of the gods of the land, their leaders could remind them that their national God was *not* a nature god of the land they dwelt in, that He was the God of a covenant Israel had entered into while wandering in the wilderness without a foot of land to call its own. They drew the contrast between the gentiles on the one hand, bound to nature, who worshiped "the sun and the moon and the stars" which God had allotted to all men, and the Israelites on the other, whom God in a moment of history had chosen "and brought forth out of the iron furnace, out of Egypt, to be unto Him a people of inheritance, as ye are this day." So almost from the beginning the people of Israel had to ask questions such as no people of the ancient world ever before considered. To what *end* had God in a certain moment of history chosen them? Was Israel properly fulfilling the mission which God had assigned it? No matter how their vision of the end that God had in mind varied in detail, the leaders of Israel always saw it as the final triumph of their Lord over the nature gods, and they regarded Israel's loyalty to Yahweh as instrumental in that triumph. Here again is no recurrent natural order of things, but a unique unrolling of the course of events that were, indeed, are, history.

From the eighth century B.C., "in the time of the breaking of nations," one great conquering people after another swept through the ancient world. Assyrians, Babylonians, Persians, Greeks, Romans in turn established themselves as masters in the area the Jews lived in. One by one the peoples of the ancient world became submerged in the succession of superstates ruled by their conquerors. They ceased to have separate identities as communities. Sometimes scattered by mass deportations, sometimes subjected to a conqueror, they gradually lost their distinctive traits as peoples. From this loss of identity the Jews were saved. They survived as a people after all their neighbors had ceased to be such because the bond of their nation was not land, the natural basis of a nation. They were bound together by history, by the sense of a past with a great historical meaning and of a future with a great historical destiny. A very insubstantial thing, the common memory or tradition of a people, proved in the end a more effective means of survival than that very substantial thing, a territory where the people could live together. Through Jesus, son of a Jewish mother, Mary, Israel transmitted its sense of historical destiny—along with much else—to Christianity.

After the fifty years of the Babylonian captivity, the eighty-one Jews were freed from thralldom by the Persian King of Kings. Their return to Jerusalem, the holy city of their God, Yahweh, and their rebuilding of the Temple that the Babylonians had wholly destroyed half a century earlier began a new era in the history of the Jews: the rebuilding of the second Temple. That era ended in A.D. 70 when the Romans destroyed forever the Temple of the Jews. This segment of *The Judaeo-Christian Tradition* will have to do with the experience of the Jews between their return to Jerusalem and the destruction of the Temple. This period, covering the return of the Jews from Babylon in 537 B.C., is called the Diaspora.

In the centuries of the Diaspora, most Jews no longer dwelt in the land which their God had promised them. Instead, they were scattered along the shores of the Mediterranean. Their outlook was restructured, as that of their ancestors had been. The Jews had to learn ways to live among people of customs different from theirs, especially with the Greeks. In 333 B.C., Alexander the Great of Macedon destroyed the Persian Empire. By means of this victory, he—and after him, his generals—had conquered the Persian Empire. For the Jews of the Diaspora, this was a fateful event. Now, for the first time, they found themselves under the domination of a people of a different culture from theirs—the Greeks. The culture of the Greeks attracted the Jews of the Diaspora, and, for a time, all of them resisted that attraction.

That resistance was embodied in Judas Maccabeus, a priest of the House of the Maccabees. The Maccabean revolt was a rising against a particular Greek tyrant. It was also a rising against the attempt of Antiochus IV to impose Greek culture on the Jews. He desecrated the Temple with idols. It was against Antiochus IV that Judas Maccabeus led the rising of the Jews. To the astonishment of the world, he overwhelmed the Syrians.

His rising resulted in many changes for the Jews and their religion. In the period known as the Diaspora, the synagogue displaced the temple as the center of religion for Jews scattered across the shores of the Mediterranean. A religion of animal sacrifice became a religion of teaching. The Jews of the Diaspora were of a different temper from the Jews of ancient Israel. For the ancient Jews, religion had been the occupation of warriors. Yahweh was Lord of Hosts, the leader of armies. The religion of

Israel was a religion of the warrior kings, of Saul and David. The Jews of the Diaspora, by contrast, cared about learning, not about warfare; they initiated the rise of rabbinical teaching in Jerusalem. From their day to this, the tradition of the Jews was to be a tradition of learning, of erudition. It was to be of the synagogue, a religion not of warriors as of yore, but of learned men, of rabbis.

In the day of the Maccabees, however, the Jews were still a warrior people, and a triumphant one. Even when they rose against the Romans, the ultimate military power of antiquity, they exemplified military heroism.

But they lost. Titus, later emperor, destroyed forever the Temple of the Jews and led them to Rome in chains. The Jews and Judaism had undergone the ultimate catastrophe: the Temple of their faith was destroyed forever. Yet before this fearsome event, a new faith had been born in Jerusalem, a faith destined to conquer the world.

Christianity had come into being in Palestine before the destruction of the Temple. In the distant future, Christians were to be the rulers of the world.

CHRISTIANITY

THE CHRISTIAN CONQUEST OF ROME

The achievement of Rome in the two centuries that followed the accession of Augustus to the Roman imperium (27 B.C.) has never been equaled. The Romans maintained peace and order in the vast world they had conquered. They protected civilization in the places where it had existed before the conquest and spread it into hitherto "backward" areas, notably into parts of Europe west of the Rhine and south of the Danube. So impressive was this achievement that, among the people of the empire, the emperor himself, in life and after death, was worshiped almost as a divinity.

The Jews refused to render this worship. So did a sect that

originated among the Jews in Palestine during the reign of Augustus' successor, Tiberius. Occasionally local officials would persecute members of this sect. They felt that people who would not do the emperor divine honors were irreligious, and the most righteous of Roman emperors, Marcus Aurelius (A.D. 161–180), thought that the sect was a danger to civilization.

Less than a hundred and fifty years after Marcus Aurelius' death, however, Constantine, sole ruler of the empire, himself became a member of that sect. His son not only adhered to it but prohibited the sacrifices that had been offered to the gods from time immemorial. By A.D. 341 this sect (called Christian after the title given its founder, Jesus, "the Christ") had become the official religion of the whole Roman Empire.

The conquest of classical civilization by Christianity is one of the wonders of history. Most religions that have spread rapidly have relied on force as a means of making converts or of gaining the support of the ruling classes, but in the first three centuries of its existence, with no organized support from the ruling class, Christianity converted a large part of the population of the Roman Empire by persuasion alone.

For Christians, the events connected with the beginnings and the early growth of their religion are—or should be—the most important things that have happened in history. Also, for students of the history of Western European civilization, whether Christians or not, the beginnings and growth of Christianity are of paramount importance. From the very beginning of Western civilization its destinies and those of Christianity were indissolubly linked. Down to our own time most of the inhabitants of the Western world have been Christian, and most Christians have lived in the Western world. Everywhere—in its practices of worship and burial, in its painting, sculpture, and music, in its literature, in its marriage and family institutions, in its philosophy and moral ideas—the Western world bears the mark of its Christian tradition. Conversely, the most vigorous and successful efforts to propagate the Christian religion during the past ten centuries have been made by the peoples of the Western world. For better or for worse, the Christian missionary in the Orient today is not likely to be identified by most Orientals with the gentle Galilean fisher for souls. He is more likely to be identified with the white men of the West, fishing for riches and power, who effected the material conquest of almost the whole earth during the last five hundred years.

What, then, was the obscure beginning of the Christian religion? How, from such a beginning, did it expand to become *the* religion of the later Roman Empire, and thereafter the religion of the Western world? To attempt an answer to these questions we must look at the later history of the Jews, for the founder and the first great propagandists of the new faith were Jews.

THE JEWS AFTER THE CAPTIVITY

The Jewish State and the Diaspora

Toward the end of the sixth century B.C., the Jews returned to Palestine. They were encouraged to do so by the Persian rulers of the latest and greatest of the ancient Oriental empires, who had conquered the Babylonian captors of the Jews. With the good will of their Persian masters, the returning Jews set about reconstructing the Temple of their God at Jerusalem. But it was only a remnant that returned. In the years since their capture in 586 B.C., many Jews had settled in the Orient—in Mesopotamia, Egypt, Persia, Asia Minor. As soldiers, farmers, and administrators they had made careers for themselves, and in large numbers they remained behind, in the places where they had settled, when some of their fellows went back to Judea. Henceforth the Jewish community was divided into two parts: the Palestinian Jews and the Jews scattered about among other peoples—the Diaspora, or Jews of the Dispersal.

From the time of the Babylonian Empire to the Roman conquest of the Near East (63 B.C.) the Jews of the Diaspora prospered and multiplied until, by some estimates, they made up as much as a fifth of the population of the Hellenistic world. These Jews inevitably made some adjustments to the communities in which they settled and took on some of the habits of life of the peoples surrounding them. The earliest known translation of the Jewish Scripture, for example, is a translation into Greek, made for Jews in Greek communities, who no longer knew the Hebrew in which their holy books were written. Yet the Jews of the Diaspora did not assimilate themselves altogether to the gentile world. They still lived by the rules of a law which inevitably set them off from their neighbors, and they still looked for leadership to the Palestinian Jewish community and to Jerusalem where the Temple was.

The Palestinian Jews had a stormy history until the Roman conquest of the eastern Mediterranean in the second and first centuries B.C. Their little land was a natural objective for all the conquerors, marching and countermarching in pursuit of their imperial designs, since Judea lay across the main lines of communication between Egypt to the south and upper Syria and Mesopotamia to the north and east. Alexander the Great of Macedon took over control of Palestine as the successor to the

Persians, and when his empire split up following his death in
323 B.C., the Jewish homeland was one of the prizes over which
the Hellenistic kings of Syria and Egypt fought. From the end of
the sixth century to the middle of the second the Jews of Palestine, indifferent to which idolatrous prince claimed dominion
over their land, submitted successively to the Persian King of
Kings; to Alexander of Macedon; to the Ptolemies, who ruled
Egypt; and to the Seleucids, who ruled the Syrian-Mesopo-
tamian Empire. Then in 168 B.C. the Hellenistic king of Syria,
Antiochus IV, drew Palestine into his scheme for tightening his
hold on his rickety empire. His aim was to bind the empire
together by strengthening those cultural traits and institutions
that had a Greek origin. When he tried to Hellenize the Palestinian Jews, however, he ran into fierce opposition that soon became a revolt under the leadership of Judas Maccabeus. The
revolt was successful, and—like local princelings elsewhere in
the decaying Syrian Empire—the family of Judas, the Hasmoneans, were able to set themselves up as independent rulers.
Members of a family of priests, they combined the offices of high
priest and king. Under them, for the first time in more than four
hundred years, a Jewish state came into being, free of outside
domination not only in religion but also in politics.

The political freedom of Judea lasted about a hundred years
from the rising of the Maccabees. A dispute over the succession
to the kingdom then led one of the aspirants along the path
habitually followed during that era by princes in the eastern
Mediterranean; he asked Rome to come to his aid. Rome followed her own habit in such matters; she found it more convenient to swallow up the disputed territory than to straighten out
the dispute itself. Thus, Judea, conquered by Pompey in 63 B.C.,

was incorporated into the Roman political system as a tributary state.

Changes in the Religion of the Jews

Before the captivity in Babylon, three elements in the religious life of Israel were clearly distinguishable: the *priestly* element, concerned especially with ceremony and the rituals of sacrifice performed in the Temple in accordance with what was believed to be God's command; the *legalist* element, centered around the Law of God, revealed in sacred writings, and concerned with the fulfillment of that Law in daily life as the way of righteousness; and the *prophetic* element, emphasizing the inward religious sense of the majesty, oneness, and goodness of God and the ethical molding of the individual and society to conform to His will.

These elements of the old religion of Israel survived the captivity and remained part of the religion of the Jews who returned to Palestine. During and after the captivity, however, several elements, not present or not so heavily stressed before, received new prominence and a new emphasis in the Judaic religion: the belief in a life beyond death, movements of asceticism or withdrawal, and the Messianic hope.

The religion of Israel before the Babylonian conquest had little to say about what, if anything, happened to men after they died. God was believed to punish the wicked and reward the righteous in this life. Meditation on the large number of unlucky righteous men and fortunate wicked ones, however, suggested that things here below did not really work out that way, and the most powerful poem in the Bible, the Book of Job, deals with the impact of suffering on a righteous man and his anguished need to know why God has so afflicted him. Gradually a great many Jews came to believe that the sufferings of the righteous would be compensated by rewards after death and that the wicked would then get the punishment that their sins had earned them.

From the time of their return to Palestine up to the period of Roman domination, thoughtful Jews gave ever more serious consideration to God's plan for Israel in history. None doubted that God would someday intervene in history to fulfill the promises He had made to His people and to justify their long-suffering faith in His love of them and in His power. At that point He would establish His rule over all men and thereby vindicate and exalt the Jews, His faithful followers and Chosen People. But the line between those physically born into Israel and those born outside did not correspond to the line between the righteous and the wicked. The iniquities of many born Jews were only too evident to the truly pious. Some of those pious Jews came to believe that the promises of God were not to all Israel, but only to the truly righteous. Amid the multitude of sinners, however, the righteous were in danger of temptation and contamination. Safety for the righteous might therefore lie in separation from the tainted doings of ordinary Jews—perhaps spiritual separation at first, marked by a special rigor and piety, but ultimately physical separation, withdrawal from the debased ordinary life of Judea by flight to and union with some special community of the pious.

It soon became clear that the ultimate triumph of Israel could not be the work of Israel. Any faint hope, aroused by the victories of the Maccabees, that the Jews could help themselves was snuffed out by the overwhelming force of Rome. Against such might there would obviously have to be some special intervention of God in history if He was to keep His promise to the Jews. Consequently the Jews came to associate the idea of the Messiah with the idea of the Great Day of the Lord, when He would establish His Kingdom or rule on earth. The Messiah was the Anointed One, chosen by God, who would come to deliver Israel from her bondage to the gentiles and rule as her King. As to how all of this would come about and how the Messiah would appear, there were all sorts of notions; some Jews believed that the coming of the Messiah would be followed by the end of history, when God would judge and destroy the wicked and resurrect the righteous dead to live with Him forever.

In the second and first centuries B.C., then, the Palestinian Jews gave much thought to their condition in this world and to the disparity between that condition and the high place in history to which they believed their God had destined them. But these Jews did not all arrive at the same conclusion as a result of their meditations. Indeed, they were a deeply divided people, split into several groups. The lines of division among three of those groups—the Sadducees, the Pharisees, and the Essenes—can be discerned fairly clearly in the tradition and the surviving historical record of the troubled time through which the Palestinian Jews were then passing.

The Sadducees, who formed the larger part of the priesthood of the Temple, appear to have been theologically conservative. They rejected the elaborate conceptions of a personal life after death that had spread among the Jews after the return from the Babylonian exile: they found no warrant for such a belief in the rather strict scripture interpretation which they favored.

The Pharisees, mainly laymen rather than priests, owed their authority to their painstaking study of the Torah, the Books of the Law, and to their skill in interpreting the Law so as to provide solutions to the problems of daily life, extending the sphere of the divine commands over the most minute actions and affairs of men. This extension required a more ample reliance on tradition and more elaborate interpretation of Scripture than the Sadducees were willing to allow. The Pharisees prided themselves on their strict conformity to the Law as they interpreted it, apparently describing themselves or being described for this reason as "the Separated Ones." Perfect conformity to the Law, however, became increasingly difficult as the Pharisaic teaching extended the rules of religious purity to cover an increasing range of everyday activities. Although the Pharisees were much admired by other Palestinian Jews, ordinary men going about their necessary business could scarcely hope to comply fully with the intricate demands of the Law. Also, unlike the Sadducees, the Pharisees accepted and propagated belief in personal immortality.

About the third Jewish group, the Essenes, little was known for sure up to a few years ago. However, the discovery of the Dead Sea Scrolls in 1947 and later may have made the Essenes the best-known segment of Palestinian Jewry in the period just before and at the outset of Roman domination of Judea. Among this collection of ancient Jewish writing, found in caves near the Wadi Qumran, a dry stream bed in the neighborhood of the Dead Sea, were the oldest surviving manuscripts of many books of the Old Testament. The Scrolls also contained rules for the governance and life of a religious community and several religious writings embodying the views of that community. The home of this community was not far to seek. On a plateau near the Qumran caves stand the ruins of an ancient habitation, Khirbet Qumran. The buildings on the plateau there were once occupied by a sect of Jews who had withdrawn from the ordinary life of the Palestinian Jewish community. In A.D. 66, the Palestinian Jews rose in revolt against Rome. Fearful that the waves of violence sweeping Palestine would reach their community, the members of the Qumran sect buried the scrolls of their library in the nearby caves. They never gathered them again; the victorious Roman troops dispersed the community, and turned the buildings of Khirbet Qumran into an army outpost. The precious library did not see light again for nearly two thousand years. In 1947, a Bedouin shepherd in quest of a stray sheep entered one of the caves and found some of the manuscripts in jars there. Since that time orientalists of half a dozen lands have worked on these scrolls and others found in the caves and among the ruins of Khirbet Qumran. They have pieced together the story of the Qumran community. From the correspondences between what they learned and what had formerly been known or conjectured about the third group of Jews, many scholars have concluded that the members of the community of Qumran belonged to that third group, the Essenes. We may at least tentatively adopt their conclusion.

Of the factions into which the Palestinian Jews were divided, the Essenes had most in common with the earlier followers of Jesus. Essene influences can be found in the New Testament, the earliest Jewish Christian communities took over a number of Essene practices, and the Essenes seem to have been favorable subjects for Christian propaganda. The Essenes probably became a separate sect, made up of rigorously pious Jews, under the Hasmoneans. Revulsion at and disillusion with the violent and degenerate heirs of the Maccabees and disappointment with the growing worldliness of the cities of Judea turned pious Jewish souls toward flight from a world that seemed hopelessly corrupt. The set of mind that pervaded the religious attitude of the Essenes, as it did that of the earliest Christian communities, may be described as apocalyptic. That is, the beliefs and rules of religious discipline of the Essenes had their foundation in the expectation that the Last Days were at hand, God's Final Judgment of the world nigh. In that time of judging, the remnant of the righteous would be saved, the sinners condemned. Like the early Christians, the Essenes, finding property meaningless in a world about to come to an end, established a sort of community of goods among the brethren. The initiation ceremony, preceding admission to the Qumran community, was a ritual bathing that was to cleanse the initiate of his sins. John the Baptist, who in the wilderness proclaimed the end of days and the coming of the Messiah and who baptized men repentant of their sins, may have been an Essene, and he certainly was familiar with their outlook and their practices. The Essenes, also, made much of the kind of ceremony which Christians called *agape,* the love feast, a meal of bread and wine, at which they ate together as a symbol of their oneness in faith and as a foreshadowing of the joyous meal they would share on the great day when the Messiah came and joined them in the feast.

The Essenes cut themselves off from the rest of the Jews of Palestine, whom they regarded as hopelessly sunk in sin and therefore doomed to destruction when the Great Day of the Lord came. On that day, long awaited and now near at hand, it would be the Essenes alone, the pure remnants of Israel, sanctified by the holy discipline they practiced and by a strict observance of the Law, who would be saved in reward for their righteousness.

Such were some of the beliefs and practices of the Essenes, as reflected in their writings. Their literature makes up one of the largest bodies of writing emanating from Palestinian Jewry in the ages of the dawn of Christianity. Their beliefs and practices are suffused with the apocalyptic spirit and the Messianic hope that attracted many Palestinian Jews to Jesus.

As we examine the situation in Palestine during the early decades of Roman rule, we are able to understand the Christian teaching about "the Fullness of Time," the conception that a unique confluence of historical events prepared the way for the coming of Jesus, for the details of his life, and for the subsequent expansion of Christianity. The poor and pious Jews of Palestine had long meditated on the great changes that God would make; and the more they thought about those great days of the Lord and longed for them, the more they came to believe that very soon God would fulfill his promises to Israel. They lived in a state of increasingly excited expectation. The excitement became only more intense as a result of the Roman conquest. The Romans were arrogant, proud, and contemptuous of God's people. Surely, many Jews felt, the Lord would not stay His hand much longer; without delay He would send the Promised and Expected One, the Messiah, to redeem and rule His people and destroy their oppressors. In the days when Augustus was laying the foundations of the new order in Rome, Judea was in ferment, ripe for revolt, waiting for a sign from God, ready for anything. It was into a Jewish world thus tense with expectation that Jesus was born in the latter part of the reign of Augustus.

THE LIFE OF JESUS

Somewhere about the twenty-seventh year of the rule of Augustus over the Roman Empire, a young Jewish woman named Mary, the wife of a carpenter, gave birth to a child, who was given the common Jewish name of Jeshua, or Jesus. The family of Jesus lived in Nazareth, a town not far from the Sea of Galilee, about sixty miles north of Jerusalem. Very little is known for certain about the early years of Jesus, or indeed about any except the last few years of his life. It seems that Jesus was born into a pious family, for he was well read, or at least well instructed, in the holy books of the Jews. It is likely that he spent some time in the local meeting places called synagogues, where the rabbis studied, explained, and interpreted the law of the Jews, and where Jews gathered for prayer. At some point in his life, Jesus himself felt a call from God to teach and preach, and to heal the diseased. In the region of Galilee his preaching attracted great crowds, and from among those crowds a small group of men attached themselves closely to him—his disciples.

No single detail of Jesus' moral teaching was absolutely new; all of it might have been found in bits and pieces in the sayings of one rabbi or another. But he did not bury his teachings under the details of legalistic reasoning. He only illustrated them with striking stories (parables) or declared them confidently as un-doubtable truth. "He spoke like one with authority," that is, like a prophet, "not as a scribe," and it was a long time since there had been a prophet in Israel. Jesus spoke with high hope of a new day at hand, of the coming of God's Kingdom on earth; of the destruction of the wicked rich, who were proud in spirit, and the redemption of the humble righteous, who were poor in spirit; of the fulfillment of God's promises to Israel. He called on those who listened to him and on the Jewish people to repent of their wicked ways and take on a new life of righteousness so that they would be ready when God's Kingdom came. As a first step he asked his hearers to believe in him—that is, in his teaching and in his divine mission. The message Jesus preached, going past the letter of the law, which ordinary men could not keep, to its spirit, profoundly moved many of the simple folk of Galilee. Even more, they were moved by his character, his powerfully attractive personality—so deeply moved that the stories of his deeds, set down in writing many years later, are still vivid and warm today.

The stir created by Jesus' preaching and the size of his following perturbed both the Roman and the Jewish authorities, fearful of any wind that might fan the smoldering discontent in Palestine into a raging flame of revolt. Perhaps the anxiety of the dominant groups, both Roman and Jewish, was heightened by rumors that some of the followers of Jesus believed him to be the Messiah, sent to throw off the Roman yoke and to rule as king over an Israel become heir to the world. Some of his followers actually did believe this, and Jesus did not specifically deny that he was the Messiah. Indeed, according to the stories about him later collected, he too believed that he was the Messiah, but his conception of the role of the Messiah differed from that of other Jews, since he felt that the Lord's Anointed was to redeem Israel and mankind, not by ruling on earth, but by suffering and dying.

In any case, at the age of about thirty-three Jesus walked into the jaws of death by leaving friendly Galilee and going with a few of his disciples to Jerusalem, the hotbed of anti-Roman feeling, during the Passover, the festival celebrating the freeing of Israel from an older bondage to Egypt. There he himself ate the Passover meal with his disciples. When he blessed and shared the unleavened Passover bread he said to his disciples, "Take, eat; this is my body." And passing the cup of Passover wine, he said, "Drink ye all of it, for it is my blood . . . which is shed for many." He frightened and angered powerful people by attacking the organization of Temple worship; he "drove the money-changers from the Temple." His presence and his actions had already aroused some of the fervent mob of Jerusalem. The fear that he might lead or precipitate a dangerous disturbance generated a conspiracy against him. One of Jesus' own disciples, Judas, betrayed Jesus into the hands of the Jewish authorities, who in turn gave him to the procurator Pontius Pilate for trial. Charged with sedition for claiming to be the King of the Jews, a claim he refused to disavow, Jesus was condemned to the death that Rome inflicted on criminals. He was nailed to a cross and left there until he died.

Although Jesus seems to have tried to warn them of what his end would be, the small band of disciples who had come with him to Jerusalem were grief stricken and horrified by this ghastly end to their hopes, hopes that their leader had come to rule the Jews and lead them to earthly victory over their enemies. Some fled back to Galilee. A pious admirer secured the body of Jesus from the authorities and buried it in a tomb. Some time later a number of the former followers of Jesus believed that they saw in the flesh, spoke to, and heard speak the man who had been placed in a tomb in Jerusalem a while before. These appearances or apparitions of Jesus, which occurred a number of times, revived the hopes of the faithful. Then Jesus ceased to appear to his followers, and they were left to make what they could of the life of their master and its meaning, with such aid as his teachings and their revived faith in him gave them. What they made of their experience of Jesus laid the foundations of Christianity.

THE PROBLEMS OF THE EARLY FOLLOWERS OF JESUS

Their belief in the resurrection—that their master was risen from the dead—ended for the followers of Jesus the despair that ensued upon his death. Thenceforth one firm conviction bound them all together: Jesus had not died in vain; he was indeed the Messiah; both his death and his resurrection were part of a divine plan. He would return, probably soon, as the Jews had long expected, to judge both the live and the dead, and to rule in glory and power as the Messiah of Israel, the Anointed One, or Christ, the Lord of All the Earth, King Jesus.

Despite this basis of common belief, the men who had put their faith in Jesus faced enormous difficulties. Most of them were simple folk with little education. They had undergone an experience that alternately depressed and exalted them, but they had meager natural gifts for expressing, defining, explaining, or interpreting that experience. All they had to go on, aside from their inward faith, was what they recalled of the words, deeds, and sufferings of Jesus. But Jesus' followers did not fully agree on the meaning of those words, deeds, and sufferings (and there never has been full agreement since), nor was it wholly clear how the teaching of Jesus bore on the situation of the disciples after his death.

The followers of Jesus who remained faithful to him were, like him, Jews. Some of them gathered in Jerusalem to await his return, because they believed that he was the Messiah, that he had returned to life from the dead and ascended to heaven, but that he would soon return to earth in glory and fulfill all the promises that they found in the Old Testament concerning the Messiah, the Redeemer of Israel. They gathered for meals, and when they broke bread together with a blessing in his name, they affirmed their special bond with him and felt his presence among them. They believed that the spirit of their Lord Jesus—the Holy Spirit or the Holy Ghost—had been sent down to them to guide them during the absence of the Master. In the meantime they must do his work. Israel, they felt, had failed to recognize the Messiah, had even brought about his crucifixion. But Israel was still the Chosen People and must be shown its error, so that when the Messiah did come again, the Jews would be ready to receive him. Indeed, if the whole pattern of history, as the disciples saw it, was to make sense, the Jews *had* to be converted before Jesus the Messiah came again in glory, since it was precisely to Israel that God had promised the Messiah. So the followers of Jesus in Jerusalem, while scrupulously obeying the law of the Palestine Jewish community, of which they were a part, sought to persuade their fellow Jews to recognize Jesus as the Christ,[1] God's anointed, the one for whom Israel had so long waited. These were the apostles—the bearers of the good tidings about the Messiah—to the Jews. Especially prominent among them were the men who shared Jesus' last supper in Jerusalem.

Their task was a hard one. Nothing that their fellow Jews had hitherto believed about the Messiah suggested that he would die the disgraceful death of a condemned criminal. Truly this was a stumbling block to the Jews, and naturally so. Nevertheless, the followers of Jesus won some adherents, not only among the Jerusalem Jews but also among the Jews of the Diaspora, who flocked to Jerusalem the holy city. The newly won followers carried the message or gospel of the risen Christ back to their homes in the Diaspora—to Antioch in Asia Minor, to Cyprus, to Rome itself. Some of the Jerusalem community went out to win followers in the smaller Jewish towns of Palestine. But it was especially in the towns outside Palestine that the new religious sect ran into the problem of the gentiles.

1. "The Christ" meant "the Anointed," from the Greek *chriein,* to anoint. The reference was to a special ceremonial rubbing with oil which was part of the induction ceremony for kings in several ancient monarchies. "Christ" was thus simply the Greek translation of the Hebrew *Messiah.* Christ Jesus means Messiah Jesus and Jesus the Christ meant Jesus the Messiah. Only gradually did *Christ* become the specific title used to designate the central figure of Christianity. By then it had ceased to bear its former special meaning of *Messiah.*

All over the Mediterranean world in the centuries before the birth of Jesus, Judaism had expanded not only by natural increase but by attracting followers among the peoples, mainly Greek speaking, amid whom the Jews were settled. Not all these gentile followers, however, were willing to make the full break with their past that Judaism required. They did not wholly accept the elaborate rules of the Jewish dietary law, which would make it impossible for them to eat with other gentiles. They did not undergo circumcision, an operation physically painful and socially drastic. They lived in a sort of spiritual halfway house, no longer attached to the gods of their fathers and their cities but still only on the outer edge of Jewry. Since they did not accept the whole Law, they could not fully take part in the life of the Jewish community. Now some of these gentiles on the fringes of Judaism were drawn to the new teaching about Jesus and began to associate themselves with his Jewish followers. The common meal was the main regular religious ceremony of those followers. If the Jewish followers of Jesus abided by the letter of Israel's law, they could not accept on an equal footing the gentiles they had won over and permit them to take part in the common meal unless those gentiles first became Jews, accepting the whole Law. The problem of what to do in this situation brought about a rift between the more conservative first followers of Jesus and the Greek-speaking group, less inclined to demand the fulfillment of the Law. The latter found a great leader in Saul of Tarsus, who later became Saint Paul.

THE LIFE AND MISSION OF PAUL

Paul was a Greek-speaking Jew of the commercial and university town of Tarsus in Asia Minor. He appears to have been well educated and to have had a fair notion of the main currents of thought in the Greco-Roman civilization of his day. He enjoyed the privilege of Roman citizenship, that is, he was under Roman law. Thus he was a far more sophisticated man, far more a man of the great world, than the first humble followers of Jesus seem to have been. Paul's formal education was Jewish. He was steeped in the literature of his people and particularly in its sacred writings. He was intensely religious, a Pharisee and, as such, a strict adherent to the Law. A man of great zeal, he regarded as blasphemous the claim of Jesus' followers that an obscure teacher who had died the ignominious death of a criminal was the Messiah whom God had sent to deliver Israel. Since Paul was a man driven to act forcefully on any conviction he held, he became a leading persecutor of the new sect.

Then, while on a persecuting mission to Damascus about five years after the death of Jesus, Paul had a vision. He believed that in that vision he saw the Son of God, the Messiah, the Christ. The vision told Paul that He, the Messiah, was the very Jesus whose followers Paul sought to destroy. Paul accepted his experience on the Damascus road as a direct communication from Christ. He believed that he had thereby been called by God Himself to be an apostle and to spread the good tidings for mankind that were the true meaning of the life, death, and resurrection of Jesus.

From that time until he disappeared from history about thirty years later, Paul became the greatest of the missionaries of the cause he had once persecuted. He traveled into Arabia, through Asia Minor, north Syria, Cyprus, Thessaly, Macedonia, and Greece, and at last, as a prisoner, he was sent to Rome itself. To the great cities of the eastern Mediterranean he carried the message that the crucified Jesus was resurrected, that he was the Messiah promised by God to the world. In his dangerous work he was beaten and whipped at least eight times, shipwrecked thrice, stoned once, imprisoned several times, and this was only the beginning of his troubles. He was sometimes prostrated by a nervous affliction. The groups he won over were quarrelsome, unstable, and difficult. And leaders of the earliest followers of Jesus distrusted Paul, disagreed with some of his deepest convictions about his own role as an apostle, and attempted to curb him and thwart his mission. In the midst of such storms and turmoil, physical, emotional, and intellectual, Paul also had to perform a colossal spiritual task—to discover the full meaning of his religious experience and discern its bearing on his mission. For Paul's mission was bound up with a broader understanding of the significance of the career of Jesus than the brotherhood of disciples at Jerusalem had imparted to it. His work had, therefore, two aspects: he cut the ties of custom and institutions that hitherto had bound the followers of Jesus to the Jews, and while he maintained the link of the new religion with the religious spirit of Israel and the God of Israel, he drastically simplified that connection. He thus made the new religion more acceptable to the gentiles and at the same time more receptive to the influence of Graeco-Roman civilization than Judaism had been.

The first aspect of Paul's work had to do with religious organization and the second with theology, or the understanding of God; yet the two were inseparably intertwined both in Paul's activity and in his thought. The result of that activity changed the history of the world. Jesus was the founder of Christianity; but it was through Paul that the Christian Church won its independence of Judaism and was made ready for its slow, steady conquest of the mind and heart of classical civilization.

The Gentile Church

In most of the towns where Paul carried on his mission—and they were many—he established communities or fellowships bound together by the message concerning Jesus, the Christ or Anointed One, as Paul preached it. Each fellowship probably had a nucleus of Jews, but in addition there were Greek-speaking gentiles who had previously been attracted to Judaism and who were now attracted by Paul's own message. The senior group of Jewish Christians in Jerusalem, directed by men who had known Jesus in the flesh, had always maintained some sort of barrier between the gentiles and the Jewish followers of Jesus, based on the distinction between those who kept the whole Law and those who did not. Paul found in such a barrier an insuperable obstacle to the full fellowship in religion that he aimed to establish among those who believed that Jesus was the Christ, and he boldly cut through it. He declared that Christ demanded of his followers neither circumcision nor obedience to dietary rules and that the gentile Christian and the Jewish Christian must be united in complete communion. At this point Paul's teaching on the conditions of Christian fellowship was indivisibly linked with his larger religious ideas. For if gentile and Jew alike were to set the Law at naught in their common life as Christians, what would be left of the Law God gave to Israel? Israel was the people of the Law, and it was to Israel that God had promised a Redeemer. How, then, could Paul promise redemption to his congregations, largely made up of gentiles, which set aside the Law? If the Messiah had not come for Israel's sake, for whose sake had He come? And for whose sake had He died?

The New Israel of Grace and Faith

Paul's answer was that Christ had come for all mankind and had died for all mankind. All mankind, Jew and gentile alike, was unrighteous, sunk in sin; in justice, all men deserved to be destroyed. The Law of the Jews and the reason of the gentiles both pointed the same way, for no Jew perfectly kept the Law of

Moses, and no gentile ever lived wholly as his reason told him was right. The efforts of the Jews, always unsuccessful, to live by the Law only showed that the Law could not make them worthy of God's love; the Law only justified His wrath: "There is none righteous, no, not one . . . for all have sinned, and come short of the glory of God." All men, Paul believed, shared his experience: "The good that I would, I do not; but the evil which I would not, that I do." The Jewish Law did not enable a man to conquer sin; it only made him more agonizingly aware of his subjection to it, of his utter inability to obey God's righteous commandments.

Since unworthy man could not save himself, out of pure mercy or grace or love—to Paul these words were synony-mous—God sent His Son to save man. The Son "became flesh," a living historical person, in the man Jesus. This was the Incarna-tion. Jesus was a perfect man, the only man who, although tempted like other men, had never sinned and therefore never deserved to suffer; yet he had suffered and died the death of a sinner on the cross. By his death *without* sin, he atoned for all the sins of man; he redeemed men from the destruction they mer-ited and made it possible for them to be saved. God let the suffering of Jesus give satisfaction for the guilt of all men and was willing, despite their sins, to let them share in the righteousness of Christ. This was the crucifixion. Thus the crucifixion brought atonement and redemption to undeserving man as a result of God's Love or Grace; its final result was man's salvation, a salvation he could never earn or deserve on his own merits. To benefit from Christ's sacrifice, however, men must acknowledge it, accept it, believe in it. The gentile who denied the true God and worshiped idols was doomed. The Jew who worshipped the true God but tried to satisfy Him by obeying the Law instead of by throwing himself on the mercy He had tendered through His

Son was also doomed. Whoever, Jew or gentile, believed in the crucified Christ might be saved; salvation was achieved through faith, not, as the Jews imagined, through adherence to the letter of the Law.

The crucified Son of God had risen from the dead and ascended to the Heavenly Father. This was the resurrection. The resurrection of Christ foreshadowed the resurrection of all the faithful on the Day of Judgment, when Christ would come again and the new age of eternal life would dawn.

The promises that God had made to old Israel would be granted to the New Israel. The old Israel of the Law, the Jews, had forfeited their right when they failed to recognize Jesus as the Messiah and turned against him. The new Israel lived by faith in Christ, not by the Law, and it comprised all, Jew or gentile, who shared in that faith. Thus Paul appropriated the ancient hopes and expectations of the Jewish nation to the new Christian Church. At the same time, he preserved for the new religion a profound conception of God that had distinguished the religion of Israel from the religions of all other ancient peoples.

The victory that God would give to the New Israel of the spirit, which had faith in Jesus as the incarnate Son of God, was not a mere earthly dominion. It was victory over the greatest enemy of all, Death.

> In a moment, in the twinkling of an eye . . . the trumpet shall sound and the dead shall be raised incorruptible. . . . Then shall be brought to pass the saying that is written, "Death is swallowed up in victory." O death, where is thy sting? O grave, where is thy victory? The sting of death is sin; and the strength of sin is the law. But . . . God . . . giveth us victory through Lord Jesus.

While it waited for the new day, the assembly of God's people, His church, whose members were those who had faith in Christ, would be guided by the Spirit of God. Those members, no longer bound by the Law of Moses, would be led in the conduct of their lives by the rule of love which they found in their hearts. God's perfect love of man, wholly gracious since man did not deserve it, would be the standard of their life, the model for their conduct with their fellows. Having become new men by the grace of God, free men no longer condemned by the Jewish law but saved by faith in Christ, they would discover that they nevertheless were able more fully and joyfully to abide by the spirit of the Law than they could when they felt themselves compelled to obey it in order to win God's love. Such, in part, was the teaching of Saint Paul.

The Historical Importance of Paul's Mission

Paul's work was already accomplished when, according to tradition, he was beheaded in Rome in about A.D. 64. He had established the new religion firmly in the gentile world of the Roman Empire, freeing it from its dependence on Judaism in general and on the center of Judaism in Jerusalem in particular. Paul had accomplished his mission none too soon. Barely two years after his death, Palestine erupted into revolt against Roman rule. After a hard campaign to subjugate the Jews, in A.D. 70 the Romans finally took Jerusalem and destroyed the Temple. The tax that Jews throughout the empire had paid for the upkeep of the Temple continued to be collected, but, rubbing salt in the wounds of the vanquished, the Romans turned the proceeds over to the treasury of the Temple of Jupiter Capitolinus in Rome. Palestinian Judaism suffered a crushing blow from its defeat, and Jewish Christianity—the Christianity of the Jews in Jerusalem—was carried along in the universal disaster. The Christians in Jerusalem had not associated themselves with the Jewish rising but had fled the city and dispersed. Here and there, off the beaten tracks of civilization, a few isolated communities of Christians who clung to the observance of the Jewish law survived—and were forgotten. Although the disaster in Palestine may have briefly shocked the Christian communities elsewhere, it did not otherwise affect them. Wholly emancipated from spiritual dependence on Judaism by their acceptance of Paul's teaching, those communities continued in their work of elaborating Christian worship, working out the organization of Christian churches, defining the Christian creed, and winning converts to the Christian faith. It is to these developments of Christianity, internal and external, in its first two or three centuries that we must now give attention.

THE DEVELOPMENT OF THE CHRISTIAN CHURCH AND CREED

The Sacraments

In the eyes of the faithful of old the Church was not just a casual gathering of people who happened to share a common belief; it was, as they said, the "mystical Body of Christ." As members of that mystical Body, Christians received from Christ, its Head, the benefits and power that led to eternal life. From the very beginning, admission to and full participation in the Church were regarded as matters of the greatest importance. Around both admission and full participation complex theories and practices grew, but the central act of admission, baptism, and of worship, communion, were built on two everyday human doings—cleansing and eating. From very early times, however, Christians held baptism and communion to be different from ordinary washing and eating because God the Father and His Son in some special way took part in them; as a consequence of this participation, they produced effects that no ordinary washing or meal could produce. It is this that is intended when baptism and communion are described as *sacraments*. They were the earliest sacraments of the church.

A whole array of meanings was attached to the ceremony of baptism. In sinking in the baptismal water, the sinner symbolically died, thus sharing in Christ's death. He emerged from the water resurrected to a new life in Christ, a Christian. The act completed his conversion. He had put off the old man and had become a new man. The waters had washed away his sins and prepared him for his new Christian existence. Baptism thus admitted men to the fellowship of the Church and marked their readiness to accept the Christian way of life. Although some parents had their children baptized in infancy, a practice encouraged by leaders in the Church, during the early centuries of Christianity most people deferred baptism. A man could have his sins washed away only once in a lifetime, and many seemed to feel that it was prudent to let their sins accumulate during the fiery years of youth and even adulthood, and wash them away by baptism at a time when, because of advanced age, one was less inclined to indulge in them again.

For organizing its worship of God the Church had a time-tested pattern in the Jewish synagogue. Prayer in common, common singing of praise to God, the reading of parts of Scripture, and the explanation of some aspect of religious truth (the sermon) were regular features of Jewish religious life. These practices were early taken over by the Christians. The center of

Christian worship, however, was a new sacrament. It grew out of the love feast or *agape,* the common meal by which Christians showed their special fellowship with one another. At the feast men partook of bread and wine as a memorial to Christ, who had given his body and blood for their redemption. The bread and wine of communion were not ordinary bread and wine; by a recurrent miracle, it was conceived, they became the very body and blood of Christ. Thus by eating the bread and drinking the wine the worshiper felt that he had united his own flesh and blood with those of Christ and so attained a most intimate union with his God. The Holy Meal—the Eucharist—not only bound each believer separately to God; it also emphasized the fellowship of Christians in the Church, for the meal was a *common* one in which Christians took part together, and a man could receive it only in and through the Church, as a member of the Christian body. The organization of the Church developed around the administration of its main sacraments—baptism and communion.

The Organization of the Church

The forms of worship of the Church developed slowly and with considerable variation from place to place. This was inevitable, since the body of Christians, scattered through the cities of the Roman world, were effectively bound together only by a common faith in Christ as Lord, and the faithful in each city made their own arrangements for worship. What was true of worship was also true of organization: a common organization emerged only gradually as a result of similar experiences and of imitation.

In the early days of Christianity, religious enthusiasm was held in highest esteem and the words of men claiming to speak under special inspiration from the spirit of God carried great weight. But inspiration and unregulated enthusiasm are dangerous foundations for an institution. It was not easy to discern false from true prophets, and inspired men of deep sincerity sometimes brought messages from the Holy Spirit that seemed contradictory.

Gradually a firmer and more regular leadership began to emerge and assume control of church affairs. The affairs of the growing body of Christians required more steady attention, more detailed work, and a more fixed outlook than was to be expected or found in inspired prophets. The place of meeting had to be acquired or rented, the money received for the poor had to be doled out, the candidates for baptism had to be instructed and questioned (catechized), arrangements for communion had to be made, and someone had to know who was eligible to receive the sacraments. The men who undertook or supervised this work were called *presbyters,* or elders, from which word comes the English "presbyter" or "priest"; some were called *episkopoi,* or overseers, from which comes the English "bishop."

By the end of the first century, in some Christian communities, the bishop was clearly distinguished from the presbyters and was their superior. The bishops eventually rested their claim to authority on apostolic succession. That is, they claimed that the original apostles had specifically appointed successors to carry on the work that Christ had entrusted to them, that these successors had in turn chosen successors, and that the bishops were therefore living representatives of the authority that Christ had transferred from himself to the apostles. The office, they held, was theirs by Christ's command, by divine right. They ruled the Church as God's chosen representatives. Especially, the bishops claimed as a matter of right to do what they had been doing as a matter of fact—to control the administration of the two main sacraments, baptism and communion. The bishops alone, they said, had the authority to administer baptism and communion, or to confer the power to administer them. This claim had a decisive influence on the character of the Church. By God's grace baptism admitted men to the band of the faithful who might be saved. By God's grace communion maintained men as true members of that chosen band. Thus the sacraments came to be regarded, not merely as channels of saving grace, but as the *only* channels, and it was held doubtful if men could be saved except through those channels. The church was thus *sacramental;* salvation came to men through the saving grace of the sacraments alone. But when the bishops claimed authority over the administration of the sacraments by divine right, the church also became *sacerdotal* (from the Latin word for priest): the means of salvation were available to the faithful only through the ministrations of a group of divinely authorized men, set above the ordinary worshiper in religious matters—the bishops and the priests.

The actual importance of the bishops tended to vary somewhat in proportion to the importance of the cities where they held office. From a very early date certain bishoprics attained a high level of eminence. The most eminent position naturally went to the bishop of Rome, the capital of the empire. Both Saint Peter, the chief among the followers of Jesus during the latter's life, and Saint Paul, the apostle to the gentiles, had come to Rome and, according to tradition, suffered martyrdom there. The Roman bishop fortified his claim to primacy within the episcopate by quoting the text in the Gospel according to Saint Matthew which reported Jesus as having said to Peter, "Thou art Peter (*petros*) and on this rock (*petra*) I will build my church."

Tradition had it that Saint Peter was the first bishop of Rome. Even before the end of the first century letters from the Roman congregation take an authoritative tone to other congregations of Christians elsewhere. By the middle of the second century at the latest the *primacy* of the see of Saint Peter was fairly generally acknowledged throughout the Church, and the position taken by the bishop of Rome on questions of doctrine and even of discipline was treated with special respect by other bishops in the West. During the third century Roman bishops claimed that the primacy which Christ bestowed on Peter implied the subordination of all Christian churches to Peter's successors, the bishops of Rome. The claim did not then gain the assent of most of the other Christian congregations. Effective papal monarchy was still a long way off, but the Roman diocese was recognized as being the special guardian of apostolic tradition, a model for other churches.

The Definition of the Christian Creed

As soon as the new religion began to win converts, it was faced with the problem of defining its creed. The Roman Empire was full of people ready to sample any new religion, men who indeed felt that this was the proper attitude toward new cults, since—who could know?—there might be something worth having in each of them. This casual attitude was alien both to Judaism and to its daughter-faith, Christianity. Those who sought admission to the Christian community of the faithful must know what the faith was, must demonstrate their understanding of it, and must confess it—that is, clearly express their acceptance of it and their rejection of any contrary belief.

The difficulty was to decide just what it was that the Christian ought to believe. In the first century and a half after the death of Jesus, the tradition about what it was right to believe was very fluid. Many who claimed to be Christians held beliefs about God and Jesus that would seem very odd to Christians today. Some believed that an imperfect God had created the world and that the Christ who redeemed it was not His Son but the Son of another and higher God who was perfect. Some held that Christ was but one among many of God's begotten sons. Others rejected the idea that the Son of God had become flesh and blood in the person of Jesus, holding that Jesus was an apparition. Others wholly or in part rejected the continuity between Judaism and Christianity and denied the divine inspiration and truth of the Jewish holy books, the Old Testament. These notions did not seem odd to second-century Christians; there was probably a time when more than half the Christians in the ancient world held religious conceptions far off the line of development later taken by Christian doctrine.

These strange and conflicting conceptions were a consequence of the rapid growth of the new religion. Men entered the Christian fold endowed with the common beliefs of the Mediterranean world. For several centuries the men of that world had been dominated by Greek speculative thought and influenced by Oriental mystery cults. As Christians, they brought with them into the Church the habits of thought and religious attitudes current in their Graeco-Oriental civilization. Much of the trouble with which those habits and attitudes afflicted Christianity resulted from the belief, very prevalent in the Hellenistic world, that matter was bad in itself and the nonmaterial good. From this conviction thoughtful Greek converts reasoned their way to many awkward conclusions:

1. The created world, being mainly material, was itself bad; therefore, it was not the work of the true God who was pure spirit, but was the creation of some other power.

2. The Son of God, pure spirit like His Father, could never have degraded Himself to the point of becoming flesh; therefore there was no true incarnation or real suffering on the cross.

3. Human evil and sin came from the material body, and salvation was the release of the immaterial soul from its bodily prison.

4. Therefore the way to salvation lay less in faith and the sacraments of the Church than in some secret or magical knowledge that would enable men to free their souls from their bodily prison, or in subduing the body and its desires by ascetic practices, such as fasting, life-long chastity, self-inflicted bodily torments.

Such beliefs the Church considered dangerous, and the development of a creed helped to prevent the admission to the Church of men who held them.

The first formulas of faith were probably very simple—perhaps involving no more than a profession of belief in the Father, the Son, and the Holy Spirit. The need to make these conceptions clear to converts who might have peculiar notions derived from non-Christian religions and philosophy led to an expansion of the Christian creed, mainly with respect to the relation of Christ to God and to man. The result was, first, the gradual definition of the doctrine of the Trinity, an effort to state in what sense God was *one, yet three,* the Father, the Son, and the Holy Spirit; and, second, an effort to define exactly in what sense the Son, who was eternal God, and Jesus, who was mortal man, were one being. The Church began struggling with these problems early and was still struggling with them about three hundred years later, when the once-despised sect had grown to be the official religion of the greatest political unit in the world, the

Roman Empire. But although the creed underwent a long course of definition, throughout most of its early history Christianity possessed explicit, if evolving, standards of faith. By those standards it distinguished its adherents from those who did not enter into its fellowship and from those who wandered beyond its boundaries. Faith came to mean acceptance of *the* faith, formulated in a creed. Excluding the unbelievers on the one hand and the heretics on the other, the church included only the orthodox, those, that is, who accepted the right teaching.

The New Testament

The Christians inherited a holy book, supposed to contain a revelation of the Divine Will. That book was the sacred writings of the Jews, the Old Testament. Believing that they were the New Israel, the heirs to the promises God had made to the Jews, Christians accepted the Old Testament as divinely inspired. But they were bound to God by a new covenant of love through Christ, and of this new covenant the old book had little to say except, Christians believed, by way of prophecy and moral instruction. Instead of a book the Christians had traditions, handed on by word of mouth, about what Jesus was believed to have said and done. Not very long after his death, however, a collection of his sayings were written down. Meanwhile, among the Christians of various cities traditional narratives of the life of Jesus, similar in general, but differing in detail, were kept alive. Soon under the influence of the Oriental religious habits of gentile converts, stories began to circulate that transformed Jesus into a great worker of magic or a demi-god. Oriental imagination also got to work on the sayings of Jesus and began to ascribe very peculiar teachings to him. The more sober Christians of the various large communities felt the need to preserve what they

regarded as the sound tradition about the life and teaching of
their Lord. One Christian community held to the basic narrative
source of the life of Jesus that now appears as the Gospel according to Saint Mark. In two other places the written sayings of
Jesus, with certain variations, were incorporated into that same
narrative or one very similar to it. The documents thus set down
became the Gospel according to Saint Matthew and the Gospel
according to Saint Luke. Finally a very different tradition, preserved probably in the great Christian center at Ephesus, was
composed into the present Gospel according to Saint John. The
first three accounts—Mark, Matthew, and Luke—were soon accepted in most Christian communities as authentic. The Gospel
according to Saint John, because it varied considerably from the
other three, was slower to win general acceptance. Eventually it
did so, but even today it is distinguished from the other three
accounts, which are called the *synoptic* gospels because of their
similar view of the events in the life of Jesus.

The letters of Paul soon achieved an authority with respect to
religious issues equal to that of the traditions about the life
and sayings of Jesus. They are, in fact, almost certainly the
earliest Christian writings to be preserved nearly in their original form. Paul wrote to the congregations of the faithful in
various places—Philippi, Corinth, Saloniki (Thessalonica), and
Rome, among others—in order to help them meet some problem of life or worship or to make clear to them his view on some
of the knotty questions the early Church had to face. Some of
these letters were kept and treasured by the community to
which Paul wrote them. Copies were sent to other neighboring
Christian groups. So powerful was Paul's influence that these
letters were soon being quoted as authoritative, and collections
were made of the letters believed to be authentic.

The acceptance of Paul's letters as authoritative opened the way to a general rule for deciding whether certain other letters addressed to various Christian churches by early Christian writers were also to be regarded as possessing some special authority. It was believed that Christ had bestowed on the apostles the gift of inspiration from the Holy Spirit and had thereby endowed their pronouncements with infallible truth. Since, however, a good many early Christian letterwriters had used the names of the apostles to lend authority to their own views, it was hard to decide whether certain letters bearing the names of the apostles actually were authentic. The churches of various communities reached different conclusions about these letters and to this day Christian churches do not agree completely on the authenticity of some of the letters. New Testament scholarship in the past century, moreover, has raised doubt about the apostolic origin of a number of previously accepted letters.

The group of accepted writings was rounded off by the Book of Revelation (the Apocalypse) and the Acts of the Apostles. The former was accepted because tradition ascribed authorship of it to the apostle John. Acts won gradual and slow recognition because it dealt with the apostles, and also because it was clearly a continuation of the accepted Gospel according to Saint Luke.

Thus there gradually emerged among the early Christian congregations a body of writings, believed to be divinely inspired, that told the history and explained the meaning of the new covenant of God with the New Israel, the Christian Church. The holy book of Christianity now had a New Testament to continue and complete the Old. Thus armed with an order of worship and sacraments, a religious organization and church officers, a creed and confessions of faith, and a holy writ, Christianity set forth on its mission.

The mission of Christianity was defined for the early Church by the last words ascribed to the resurrected Jesus in the Gospel according to Saint Matthew. There he is reported to have said to his disciples: "Go ye therefore, and teach all the nations, baptizing them in the name of the Father and of the Son and of the Holy Ghost; teaching them to observe all things whatsoever I have commanded you." The mission of the Church, then, was to convert the world to Christianity. The little band of Christians did not hesitate to undertake this seemingly preposterous effort. That Jesus was able to turn men to devote their lives to so discouraging a task is evidence of the remarkable power of his personality.

CHRISTIANITY AND THE ROMAN EMPIRE

We have already learned of the earliest steps taken to win the world to Christianity: the first, and on the whole unsuccessful, efforts to gain followers among the Palestinian Jews, the more successful attempts to convert the Jews of the Diaspora, and the beginnings made by Paul toward bringing gentiles—the mass of non-Jewish inhabitants of the empire—into the Christian fold. The early expansion of Christianity took place primarily along the great trade routes and in the big commercial towns of the Roman Empire—Antioch, Ephesus, Smyrna, Corinth, Saloniki, Rome, and, before the end of the second century, Alexandria, Lyon, and Carthage. From these urban centers Christianity spread into smaller places and, more slowly, among the people of the countryside. The resistance of the country population to the message of the Gospel has left its mark on language: non-Christians are called *pagans,* a word that originally meant simply "inhabitant of the countryside"; the word "peasant" is ultimately derived from the same root. Yet in some places the conversion of country folk was well underway early in the second century.

The spread of Christianity through the language groups of the empire to some extent paralleled its spread from great cities to lesser towns and finally to the countryside. Except for a few Palestinian Christian Jews, early Christians spoke Greek. And in the Hellenistic world, after the Roman conquest as before, Greek was the language of the cities, while the village folk of the conquered Orient held to their local dialects or to some widespread Semitic tongue, such as Syriac or Aramaic. It was only slowly that Greek-speaking Christianity, born of a people of Semitic speech, learned to address the mass of people in west Asia in their native Semitic languages.

In the western part of the empire matters were even more complicated, for there it was necessary to crack through three and in one case four language barriers to reach all the people. In this vast area a wild variety of native tongues was overlaid by Latin. But in the West, as in the East, Christianity, working out from the communities of Hellenistic Jews, for a long time used Greek. The "Romans" to whom Saint Paul addressed his most famous letter were clearly not Roman Romans but a Greek or Greek-speaking Jewish colony settled in the capital. Indeed, although the Christian community in Rome may have existed two decades after the crucifixion, it produced no significant Christian literature in the Latin tongue for at least a century. At Carthage in the Roman province of Africa, where the earliest important Christian writings in Latin appeared, the propagation of Christianity first had to break through Latin resistance to a Greek-speaking religion, then to Punic (Phoenician) resistance to a religion of Latin intruders. Even when the Punic peoples had been won over, there was still the native population—the Berbers—to be reached. Despite these obstacles the Christian faith spread beyond the Mediterranean world. Within the Roman Empire it extended into the hinterland of Western Europe as far as the remote isle of Britain. In the East it stretched beyond the bounds of the empire into Mesopotamia and Armenia.

The mission of Christianity did not enjoy support or protection from the Roman state. For almost three hundred years it was regarded by the authorities with distrust. Its followers suffered occasional persecution, and sometimes that persecution was intense, thorough, and violent.

The official attitude of the Roman state on Christians was direct and forthright. It was not a question of what Christians believed or how they lived. They could believe or live as it suited them provided that they stayed within the law. For the classical world religion was not primarily a matter of belief, but of participation in rites and ceremonies, and if people lived in a manner contrary to the law, the law could take care of that. As a proof of their loyalty, the state sometimes imposed on individuals the obligation to offer sacrifice before the images of the gods and of the living emperor. To refuse these simple acts was to deny the reverence due the empire and the divine forces protecting it. A man was free to doubt the existence of the gods, but to refuse to make the sacrifices seemed to indicate indifference to what general opinion regarded as the interests of the public. By his refusal a man proclaimed himself an enemy of the state, and such a one must die. The Christians, of course, could not obey this rule any more than the Jews could. Their customs were the same as those of the Jews on this matter, for their God was the same, and they were under His express commandment to have no other god and to bow down to no graven images. In this matter the Jews, however, received exceptional treatment from Rome because they were a nation, and the Romans did not willingly interfere with the ancient customs of conquered people, even customs so eccentric and repulsive to the Romans as those of the Jews. The Christians, however, were no nation in Roman eyes. They were just a religious cult like dozens of others, and they had to abide by Roman law.

The price that Rome exacted for such obstinacy was death. Nevertheless, the Romans seem not to have engaged in a general persecution of Christians during the first two centuries after the crucifixion. Provincial administrators treated Christians under their jurisdiction as their consciences, their prejudices, and the situation in each province suggested. A systematic hunting out of Christians rarely, if ever, took place. In general, Christians had less to fear from Roman officials than from the local mobs who hated them for their rejection of the old gods and the old ways of religion. Nevertheless, in the empire as a whole over the period of two hundred years, many Christians testified to their faith by dying as martyrs for it, whether at the hands of mobs or at the hands of Roman officials carrying out the orders deemed necessary to maintain the majesty of the empire.

The last great effort to organize the life of a vast world-state on the classical pattern of the good life ended with the death of Marcus Aurelius (A.D. 180). During the next century, the Roman Empire underwent a series of economic and political crises that shook its very foundations. Up to the death of Marcus Aurelius the influence of the Orient in the empire had been kept within bounds. The weakening of imperial organization dropped the barriers. Eastern influence flooded in, especially in the matter of religion, and of these influences by far the most powerful, most purposeful, and best organized was Christianity. But of all the religions of the East, Christianity was the one from which the old Roman way of life had most to fear.

It was probably the very success of the Christian mission that instigated the first general Roman persecutions, under Decius (249–251) and Valerian (253–260). These emperors, engaged in a struggle with the Goths and the Persians, doubtless considered that civilization itself, as they understood it, was at stake in the conflict. While they struggled on the frontiers, the Christians seemed to be undermining the home front by refusing the reverence due to the emperor and the gods—the chief props of the empire. Christians were also notoriously averse to military service. To Decius and Valerian, they must have appeared to be compounding treason with blasphemy. Their sufferings under the general persecution were great, but these did not last long, ending with the death of the two emperors. The Christians had grown stronger and more numerous; the very steadfastness of many of them in the face of death won many new converts to the faith. Almost a half-century of peace and rapid expansion for the Christian Church followed the death of Valerian. Then came the last and greatest persecution initiated by the Emperor Diocletian (284–305). This resolute soldier took drastic measures to restore to life an empire suffering from economic anemia, trying to draw all the resources of the Roman world to support the structure of state and army. On the terms that Roman emperors since the beginning had demanded—participation in the sacrifices—Diocletian could not win active support for his work from the most powerful moral and religious force in the empire—the Christian Church. He aimed to destroy that force and therefore unleashed a persecution more systematic, more intense, and more thorough than any the Christians had had to endure before.

Diocletian did not succeed in having done with the Christians before he retired and died. He had come short of his purpose, as the Roman state itself had come short throughout the history of its relations with Christianity. For two hundred and fifty years the empire had failed to force the Christian Church to accept its terms. Now the empire began a search for new terms that the Church would accept. In its perilous condition after the disasters of the third century, the empire could no longer afford to treat as an internal enemy the most effectively organized body of men within its boundaries. The empire could not lick the Christians, so it looked for ways to join them. This search for a new relation with the Christian Church went on for a hundred years after the retirement of Diocletian. For almost three centuries, Christians had lived as outlaws in Roman society, and they had adapted their organization and attitudes to the world to the condition of outlawry. Their leaders had given little thought to the terms on which the Church could collaborate with the empire, and until the beginning of the fourth century the leaders of the empire had given no thought at all to the problem of collaboration with the Christian Church. It soon became clear, however, that arrangements for collaboration necessarily implied a great change for the empire and even more drastic changes in the Christian Church itself.

The story of how Church and empire adjusted to their new and difficult relationship lies beyond the scope of this volume. Here we must briefly discuss the most tantalizing question of all—how can one explain the astonishing rags-to-riches story of the Christian Church? What enabled a small Jewish sect to become in about three hundred years the official religion of the whole Roman Empire?

THE APPEAL OF EARLY CHRISTIANITY

Religion in the Roman Empire

The triumph of Christianity was a triumph over *all the alternative forms of religious activity and all the alternative ways of understanding God, the world, and man* that were current in the Roman Empire in the first three centuries of our era. The distinction between "forms of religious activity" and "ways of understanding" had a special significance in classical civilization. In our own day if we ask a man what his religion is, we expect his answer to tell us something both about what he believes and about how he worships; ceremony and belief go hand in hand. It was otherwise with most men in the Graeco-Roman world. The gods they worshiped were guardians of particular places: of the hearth, of the household, of the clan, of the city, of the peoples. Or they watched over certain activities—traveling, or speaking, or planting, or harvesting, or sleeping. What men ordinarily believed about such gods was simply that they were the "powers in charge," and that in undertaking any important action, individual or collective, it was sensible to invoke the support of the appropriate god or gods, to satisfy their vanity with processions, to build them fine houses, or temples, to feed them with sacrifices, to get their advice—if they happened to be the advice-giving sort—from their priests, and to express gratitude to them by means of special ceremonies when projects under their protection prospered. If the gods of foreign people seemed to have anything to offer, they were hospitably received by the Greeks and Romans, either by assimilation or by addition. Thus Sabazios, a rough storm god of Asia Minor, became Zeus Sabazios by virtue of his functional similarity to the Greek thunder god. The best-known instance of such assimilation took place between the gods of Rome and of Greece, an assimilation that to this day confuses the schoolboy: the Greek Hephaestos is the Roman Vulcan, Greek Hermes is Roman Mercury, Greek Aphrodite is Roman Venus, and so on. Some foreign deities were too fully equipped with well-defined identities (in the form of myths) to be merged with the local gods. In such cases the foreign deity was simply given a place alongside the other gods. If people turned to the foreign god for help he prospered; otherwise he did not. He was pretty much on his own. Two goddesses especially, Egyptian Isis and Phrygian Cybele, made good in the Graeco-Roman world.

Religion in the Roman Empire, then, consisted largely of the rites and ceremonies performed for certain powerful beings to get their favor in the affairs of the individual, of the family, and of the larger associations of men, all the way up to the empire itself. If we ask what ordinary people thought about religion, the answer seems to be that they did not think about it or even regard it as a subject for thought. Popular religion had neither creed nor theology.

The people who did think about the gods and religion were the philosophers. Few philosophers since the fourth century B.C. had really taken seriously the myths of the gods or—as separate beings—the gods themselves. The most influential philosophers in the Graeco-Roman world were the Stoics. The Stoics were persuaded that there was one divine being, a universal reason, and they called this being God. The rational laws of this being were the source of order in nature: they were the laws of nature. By their possession of reason men were linked to this rational God in a single universal community or commonwealth. It was their reason that enabled men to know the laws of nature and to distinguish right, which was obedience to those laws, from wrong, which was disobedience. The good citizen of the universal commonwealth conformed to the laws of nature, the bad citizen was led to disregard them by the passions and desires of the body. Control of the passions was the task of reason. A man attained the good and godly life when he had subjugated his bodily passions to his rational mind and thus lived in accord with the laws of nature. Stoic philosophy, with its solid emphasis on practical virtues and the sober conduct of life, appealed strongly to many of the most important men in the Roman Empire—to leading administrators and jurists. One of the emperors, Marcus Aurelius, was himself a Stoic philosopher and set down a book of *Meditations* in a Stoic vein. Insofar as the upper classes in the empire can be said to have had a religion that religion was philosophy—Stoic or other.

It was to both kinds of Graeco-Roman religiousness—the kind that was bound up with pious rites to the gods and the kind that was worked out as philosophy—that Christianity had to make its appeal.

The Heritage from Israel

Christianity started its career with certain powerful advantages. The god of pagan philosophy was a chilly abstraction, remote and inactive. The Christian God was a God of Right, as the philosopher's God was; but he was also a God of love and mercy, forgiving and gracious as well as just. He *cared* in a very personal way about man. At the same time he was all-powerful. The gods of popular religion had their spheres of power, more or less extensive, but limited by each other and by the ordinary rule of Fate, or Fortune, in man's affairs. The Christian God had no such limits, for there were no other gods. He was the creator and ruler of all that was. Whatever happened happened according to

His will, and nothing ever happened against His will; and that Divine Will was also loving, ultimately turned toward good for all men. Such a full and profound sense of the divine could attract both the minds of philosophers and the hearts of humble folk.

The Christians were *one* people—God's Chosen People by adoption, as Israel had been His Chosen People by inheritance—a close-knit community bound together in fellowship based on love of God and brotherly love: "Thou shall love the Lord thy God with all thy heart and thy neighbor as thyself." For early Christians these words from the Old Testament were more than a ritual formula. They were the First Command of God. The fellowship of Christians showed itself in mutual support in adversity, in generous giving to the poor brethren, in provision for widows and orphans, in the hospitality that a traveling Christian might find among his fellow Christians in a strange town. The fellowship was one of religious equality. God made no worldly distinction of persons, of rich and poor, slave and free. All Christians must extend the hand of fellowship to their brethren of every degree.

The Christian moral standard—derived from the rigorous ethical requirements of the Law of Israel—was high, as high as the demands of Stoic philosophy. It made those demands not merely on philosophers but on all believers. The Church provided a series of simple and direct, though austere, rules for the conduct of life to people, most of whom had lived by no such elevated code before. And although it censured and punished Christians who broke the rules, it learned to forgive—as it believed God did—the repentant sinner.

Finally, Christianity, like Judaism, required conversion. One could not simply add the cult of Christ to the cults of all the other gods for whatever advantage there might be in performing the required ceremonies. To turn *to* Christ was to turn *away* from the old gods, to take on a new life with new responsibilities and a new meaning. Even before the rise of Christianity many men had begun to feel dissatisfied with the old gods. From the end of the second century A.D. the empire began to decay, and since the protection of the empire was their principal job, the old gods lost status. It was from then on easier to turn to the Christian God for help, for rescue, for security against the gnawing of anxiety. But the demand for *conversion to* rather than mere *adoption of* Christianity assured the steadfastness of the new adherents. The bond linking men to the new faith was much stouter than that which had bound them to the old gods. Many converts renounced their Christianity in periods of intensive persecution. Yet amid its many problems the early Church did not have to worry much about Christians having a change of heart and returning to the old gods. Its problem lay rather with the many folk who, having renounced their faith to save their skins, hastened to resume it again to save their souls.

Christianity shared with Judaism all these traits—a profound vision of God, a rigorous standard for the conduct of life, a highly organized community life in synagogue or church, and the requirement of conversion. Yet, although Judaism made some efforts to win the world for the God of Israel, its achievements, while considerable, were far short of what the Christians attained. The difference in success probably resulted in part from differences in the Jewish and Christian requirements for conversion. Men attracted by the powerful religious message of Judaism were repelled by the minute and exacting requirements of the Jewish law. That law, submission to which was required for conversion, wholly cut the convert off from all his old social ties, since to give hospitality to a gentile or receive it from him without breaking the laws of ritual purity was very difficult. And as if to make the difficult impossible, to raise an insurmountable barrier against their own mission, the Jews demanded circumcision as a part of conversion.

Despite such difficulties the powerful attraction of Judaism had won it many converts in the Roman world. By rejecting the ceremonial law and retaining only the moral law, by replacing the demand for circumcision of the flesh with the requirement of a change of heart, Christianity got rid of the obstacles that turned men away from Judaism, while it appropriated for its mission those aspects of Judaism that the gentiles found most attractive. A man could enjoy inward renewal, a solid code of conduct, the fellowship of other Christians, and the spiritual support of the Christian vision of God without having entirely to reorder and change the whole of his social relationships drastically.

The Christian Contribution

Christianity had a universal appeal in the days of imperial Rome, universal in the sense that it drew to it some adherents from every stratum of society, every walk of life. Some elements in that appeal it shared with other Oriental cults. These cults grew simultaneously with Christianity because in some measure the cults and early Christianity appealed to emotional needs that were widespread among the inhabitants of the Roman world in the era of its expansion.

The desire for membership in a group affording mutual aid and support, which gave to ancient cult associations much of their attractiveness, the desire for insurance against an uncomfortable or shadowy hereafter, the wish to secure a powerful supernatural protector who could bend for your benefit the decrees of fate, the craving for some sort of plus-value, the eager curiosity for revelation—all these were operative in the advance of both Christianity and the Oriental mystery cults. So was the desire for some sort of effective rite, for some denial by act of man's helplessness. The men who followed the Christian way were not so different from the men who followed the pagan.

It is true that Christianity was in some measure bent to the shape of the late classical world, as it has since been bent to the shape of other civilizations in various stages of their history. This is only to say that Christianity, like any other religion, had to stoop to conquer. Yet it will not do to overemphasize the similarities of Christianity to the Oriental mystery cults. For one thing, Christianity stooped to conquer and conquered; some of the Oriental religions, in effect, stooped and were conquered. They adapted so well to late classical antiquity that their deities were practically absorbed by the gods of Graeco-Roman paganism. There were even movements that tended to perform a like operation of absorption on Christianity and the God of the Christians, but the danger of absorption was not so great. Both the sense of absolute separateness from other cults that Christianity inherited from Israel and the historical base of the Christian creed prevented an amalgamation of Christianity with the religion of the gentiles. There was not really much chance that alongside Jupiter and Mars, Isis and Cybele and Mithra, Christ would take one place among many in an expanded pantheon.

Nor does it seem that Christianity borrowed from the mystery religions of the Orient as extensively as it was once believed. Much that used to be thought of as coming to Christianity from the common stock of the Oriental cults now appears to have had its roots in Jewish religious tradition of the first two or three centuries before the birth of Jesus. We have already seen that the belief in a godsent redeemer, the sacramental washing, and the sacramental meal have Jewish antecedents; in fact they appear in Christianity before its contact with the gentile world could have significantly affected its outlook.

The parallels between Christianity and the Oriental mystery religions are nevertheless highly significant. The remarkable fact is that in each instance the Christian practice or rule or rite possessed some peculiarity that was ultimately to its advantage in its rivalry with all other late classical forms of religious expression. Thus, for example, the Church promised salvation to those who adhered to it in the right way. Other Eastern cults offered salvation too, and so did a Greek religious philosophy called neo-Platonism. But the cults were often rather secret affairs, while neo-Platonism, like all Greek philosophy, made salvation an intellectual achievement, available therefore only to the educated and, in effect, to members of the leisure class, or the well-to-do. The gates of salvation through the Church, on the other hand, were open to all, and neither wealth nor knowledge nor intellectual prowess counted for anything, but only steadfastness of faith and decency of conduct. Especially sexual difference did not count. This was of particular importance in the ancient world. The most successful oriental cult, except for Christianity, was Mithraism, a modification on a considerable scale of the religion of ancient Persia. But Mithraism was a religion for men only. Hence it appealed powerfully to soldiers, but, naturally, it did not appeal at all to women. The handicaps under which Mithraism labored in the contest with Christianity were manifest: it declared half the human race ineligible for participation in its rites and its benefits.

Other cults had special rites of initiation and communion

corresponding to the Christian baptism and Holy Eucharist, but again the cult rites tended to be exclusive and expensive. In the *taurobolium,* an important rite of initiation in several of the cults, for example, a bull was slaughtered so that its blood fell on the communicant. Aside from any squeamishness a man might feel at the notion of being drenched in fresh bull blood, to enjoy the benefit of this particular rite one had to be able to afford to waste a bull. By contrast, a man could enter the Christian fold by baptism and renew his communion with his God in the sacrament of the Eucharist simply and at very little material cost. Thus in its rites as well as in its teachings Christianity had special attractions for the earnest poor. And, of course, most of the city people of the empire were poor.

The myth of a god who died and was revived for the good of the world was very old at the beginning of the Christian era. Adonis and Osiris, who were killed and rose again, had long been the centers of cults around the Mediterranean. The Christian idea that the Son of God had suffered death for man and then been resurrected was therefore quite congenial to many people of the Roman world-state. None of the other gods of the Oriental cults, however, was supposed to have existed in the same way that human beings exist, in the stream of historical time. But the whole story of the Christian redeemer was tied up with historical events, with what was supposed to have happened in Palestine in the reigns of Augustus and Tiberius to a man named Jesus. In this respect the Christian divine redeemer wholly differed from the redeemers in other cults; he was not mythical and timeless; *he happened in history.*

The involvement of its divine redeemer in historical doings at first was a handicap to the Christian Church; it was, as Paul said, "foolishness to the Greeks." For Romans of the first Christian century there was no need for a messiah to give history (and therefore human life) a meaning, because the Emperor Augustus had already done that. He had saved the world and civilization from universal war and barbarism. To many thoughtful men in the first two centuries of the Christian era the Roman Empire seemed to be the fulfillment of history, the end toward which it had long been moving. Rome was eternal, and life was unthinkable without it.

But in the midst of the disasters of the third century it seemed that Rome was dying. Since they had been paid, as it were, in sacrifices, ceremonials, and temples, to protect the empire, most of the gods of the Graeco-Roman world were involved in the disasters of the empire. The Christian God, however, was unhurt by the troubles of the empire, since He had never been one of its gods. Moreover there was connected with the Christian God a conception of the meaning of history quite independent of anything that might happen to the Roman Empire. For Christians, history focused on man's fall from grace, his redemption by Christ's suffering and death, and the Last Judgment, when those who had faith would be saved and the rest condemned. Since the Christian view of history did not stand or fall on the survival of merely human institutions, Christians did not feel that the collapse of Rome deprived the world of meaning. And, when disillusion came, men who had pinned their faith and hopes on the empire could find a new center for faith and hope in Christianity.

Thus it was that Christianity won great numbers of adherents in its first three centuries, despite the hostility of the state. Yet in the year A.D. 300 by no means half, probably not even a quarter, of the inhabitants of the Roman world were Christians. By A.D. 400 most of the population of that world was at least nominally Christian. This last vast wave of conversions was not a "natural" or spontaneous movement. It had the armature of the Roman state behind it. The empire finally became Christian under the impulsion of Christian emperors. Christians who relied on—put their faith in—princes for the defense, support, and propagation of their religion had to rethink and, ultimately, radically revise the relations of the Church to "the powers of this world," that matrix of men and their deeds which the founders of Christianity had so willingly renounced. The new orientation of the Church, its attempts to achieve a symbiosis with the empire, opened a new period in its history, a new era in the development of the Judaeo-Christian tradition, and it makes a suitable stopping place for this book.

SELECTED
BIBLIOGRAPHY

INTRODUCTION TO COMPARATIVE RELIGION

Students who want to look further into subjects introduced in this book might begin with a consideration of some of the problems raised by the study of the history of religion. The following books provide some insight into the comparative method and suggest how various scholarly disciplines—such as archaeology, sociology, anthropology, history, and philosophy—can be combined in order to reconstruct past religious experiences.

Berger, Peter L., *The Sacred Canopy: Elements of a Sociological Theory of Religion* (Doubleday, 1967), perhaps the most influential work on the sociology of religion in the last two decades.

Eliade, Mircea, *Cosmos and History: The Myth of the Eternal Return* (Harper & Row, 1959).

———. *Patterns in Comparative Religion* (Meridian, 1963). Eliade is one of the great scholars of comparative religion. His books are full of interesting information and suggestive analogies between religious traditions, but his arguments are often difficult for the beginner to follow.

Kee, Howard Clark, *Miracle in the Early Christian World: A Study in Sociohistorical Method* (Yale University Press, 1983).

Levy, G. Racher, *Religious Conceptions of the Stone Age and Their Influence upon European Thought* (Harper & Row, 1963), an introduction to the problem of reconstructing past religious experiences from archaeological evidence; well written and exciting.

Wach, Joachim, *The Comparative Study of Religions* (Columbia University Press, 1961).

——. *Sociology of Religion* (Phoenix, 1958). Wach's approach to the study of religion is sociological, which means that he is more interested in finding parallels and similarities in the forms of religious organization and expression than differences between the great religious traditions. His works are well suited for the beginner, however, for they define clearly the main types of religious thought and action.

THE CULTURES OF THE ANCIENT NEAR EAST

The study of a specific religious tradition always entails consideration of the degree to which that tradition is purely original or whether it is primarily derivative. So too with ancient Judaism. Was Judaism a typical ancient Near Eastern religion similar to those normally found in Mesopotamia or Egypt? In what respect does Hebrew ethical monotheism resemble the solar monotheism of the Egyptian New Kingdom? Were Hebrew religious institutions borrowed from the peoples with whom they came into contact during their early wanderings? And if so, which was the dominant influence—Mesopotamia or Egypt? Some of these questions are dealt with directly in the works listed below.

First, the student might consult some works of a general nature that provide an introduction to the entire sweep of ancient Near Eastern historical development.

Childe, V. G., *What Happened in History* (Pelican, 1957), a materialistic analysis of the rise of ancient civilization, giving special emphasis to technological changes as factors in the rise and fall of civilizations. Childe's book can be read profitably by most students, although the wealth of detail sometimes obscures the main line of argument.

De Burgh, W. G., *Legacy of the Ancient World* (Penguin, 1963), a traditional general history of the ancient world. A very good introduction, but it should be supplemented by political accounts, since De Burgh concentrates on cultural development.

Moscati, Sabatino, *Ancient Semitic Civilizations* (Capricorn, 1960), a somewhat sketchy survey of the rise and fall of Semitic cultures in the ancient Near East, but it will provide the beginning student with the basic facts.

The following works deal with the religious and cultural matrix within which and against which ancient Judaism defined itself.

Albright, F. W., *From the Stone Age to Christianity* (Anchor, 1957), a provocative and learned work by the dean of American Biblical archaeologists. Students are advised to pass over the philosophical introduction to the author's philosophy of history.

Breasted, J. H., *Development of Religion and Thought in Ancient Egypt* (Harper & Row, 1959), an intriguing analysis of the mind of ancient Egypt by a scholar who sometimes took liberty with the texts in order to force a similarity to Biblical style.

Frankfort, Henri, *Ancient Egyptian Religion: An Interpretation* (Harper & Row, 1961), by one of the foremost experts of the ancient Near East; well written, intense, and up-to-date in scholarship.

———. *Birth of Civilization in the Near East* (Anchor, 1956), deals with the emergence of civilization in the Tigris-Euphrates Valley and the expansion of civilization into India and Egypt. Establishes the matrix and pattern of change within which Israel emerged.

Frankfort, Henri, et al., *Before Philosophy* (Penguin, 1961), a collection of brilliant essays analyzing the institutions and myths of ancient Egypt and Mesopotamia and describing the evolution of the ancient mind from myth to religion and philosophy; difficult but rewarding for the student who works through them.

Greenspahn, Frederick E., ed., *Essential Papers on Israel and the Ancient Near*

East (New York University Press, 1991), a collection of seventeen previously published essays on the interrelationship between ancient Israel and its Near Eastern environment.

Wilson, John, *The Culture of Ancient Egypt* (Phoenix, 1957), a superbly written study of the relation between the Egyptian land and the institutions and ideas of ancient Egyptian culture. The scholarship is of the highest order, but this book can be read profitably by any student.

INTERNAL EVOLUTION OF JUDAISM FROM THE EXODUS TO THE EXILE

The main questions which ought to be considered here are: How did the ancient Hebrews manage to overcome their tribalism and unite into a single people under a king? What was the role of the priesthood in the monarchy? What were the dominant stresses and strains on the monarchy? Why did the Jews split into two kingdoms after the death of Solomon? What was the role of the prophets in trying to effect the reunification of Israel? How did the disappearance of the Jewish state affect the teachings of the prophets? What was the effect of the Exile on the Jews' conception of their chosenness?

Albright, F. W., *The Biblical Period from Abraham to Ezra* (Harper & Row, 1963), surveys the history, culture, and religion of ancient Israel, accounts for the increasingly spiritualist character of the Hebrews' conception of their god, and anticipates the emergence of the messianic tradition during the Exile.

Baeck, Leo, *Essence of Judaism* (Schocken, 1948), deals essentially with rabbinic Judaism but probes the essence of the religion as it emerges in the exile period.

Ben-Sasson, H. H., ed., *A History of the Jewish People* (Harvard University Press, 1989), an encompassing historical account, written by leading Israeli scholars, of the Jewish experience from ancient times to the present.

Buber, Martin, *Moses: The Revelation and the Covenant* (Harper & Row, 1958), an attempt to reconstruct the figure of Moses, to deal with the events of the Exodus, and to establish the bases of ancient Judaism; the work of a great Jewish philosopher.

Driver, S. R., *Introduction to the Literature of the Old Testament* (Meridian, 1962), an old work, originally published in 1900, but still exciting for its insights into the literary impact of the various books of the Old Testament.

Epstein, Isidore, *Judaism* (Penguin, 1959), a frankly conservative approach to the history of the Jews, especially in its handling of the Old Testament period.

Friedman, Elliott, *Who Wrote the Bible?* (Harper & Row, 1987), despite its popular-sounding title, this is a work of solid scholarship summarizing current views on the environment in which the Bible emerged and problems of authorship.

Meek, T. J., *Hebrew Origins* (Harper & Row, 1960), an exceedingly learned, highly condensed, provocative, and well-argued attempt to distinguish between those elements of early Hebrew culture that were borrowed from other peoples and those that were original creations of the Jews; essentially a political interpretation of some of the splits in early Hebrew culture, based on the assumption that the Joseph tribes alone went to Egypt, leaving a large body of Hebrews behind who succumbed to Canaanite influences. Much of the argument is based on philological evidence, but the argument can be followed even without a knowledge of Hebrew.

Mendenhall, G. E., *The Tenth Generation: The Origins of the Biblical Tradition* (Johns Hopkins University Press, 1973), a fascinating and clear description of the history of Israel and the development of the Hebrew Scriptures.

Oesterley, W. O., and T. H. Robinson, *Introduction to the Books of the Old Testament* (Meridian, 1958), provides information about the historical background against which the various books of the Old Testament took shape; high scholarly competence and well written; a good introduction.

Rowley, H. H., *Growth of the Old Testament* (Harper & Row, 1963), an account of changing opinion on the date and authorship of the books of the Old Testament.

Thomas, D. Winton, ed., *Documents from Old Testament Times* (Harper & Row, 1961), translated and edited by members of the Society for Old Testament Study; introductions and bibliographies are good.

Wellhausen, Julius, *Prolegomena to the History of Ancient Israel* (Meridian, 1957), a great classic in Judaic studies, originally published in 1878 but still worth reading.

POST-BIBLICAL JUDAISM

For the history of the ancient Hebrews after their return from exile the main questions are: What were the effects of the Exile on Jewish religious thought? What attempts were made by the Jews to re-establish a state in Palestine after their return? Why did these attempts fail? What were the effects of the political failure? Does the absence of an independent Jewish state account for the influence of non-Jewish religious traditions that appear in Jewish writings during this period? What was the nature of messianism after the return from the Exile? In what sense did the post-Exilic Jewish experience prepare the way for Christianity?

There are a number of editions of the documents for this period. General collections are:

Baron, S. W., and J. L. Blau, eds., *Judaism: Post-Biblical and Talmudic Period* (Library of Liberal Arts, 1954).

Barrett, C. K., ed., *New Testament Background: Selected Documents* (Harper & Row, 1961).

Cohen, Shaye J. D., *From the Maccabees to the Mishnah* (Westminster Press, 1989), a historical account of the Jewish people and religion during the transitional period from the Graeco-Roman to the early rabbinic period.

Grant, F. C., ed., *Hellenistic Religions: The Age of Syncretism* (Library of Liberal Arts, 1953).

Holtz, Barry, ed., *Back to the Sources: Reading the Classic Jewish Texts* (Summit Books, 1984), contains accessible introductions, written by specialists, to the central works of the Jewish tradition, including the Hebrew Bible, Talmud, and Midrash.

Neusner, Jacob. The voluminous, provocative, and controversial writings of Jacob Neusner should be consulted on various aspects of rabbinic Judaism and its literature. This huge corpus includes new translations and editions of classical texts, detailed textual studies, and broad syntheses.

Schiffman, Lawrence, *From Text to Tradition: A History of Second Temple and Rabbinic Judaism* (Ktav, 1991), written by a leading Dead Sea Scrolls scholar, this surveys the various manifestations of Judaism in the Graeco-Roman period and illuminates the context in which Christianity emerged.

Smith, M., *Palestinian Parties and Politics That Shaped the Old Testament* (Columbia University Press, 1971), a good survey of the forces at work behind the writing of the Hebrew Scriptures.

Urbach, Ephraim, *The Sages: The World and Wisdom of the Rabbis of the Talmud* (Harvard University Press, 1987). An encompassing survey of the doctrines of rabbinic Judaism.

Editions of works on and translations of the Dead Sea Scrolls include:

Allegro, J. M., *The Dead Sea Scrolls* (Penguin, 1956), a popular account of the Qumran community, the contents of the scrolls, and a somewhat sensationalist evaluation of their significance for the history of Christianity.

Danielou, Jean, *The Dead Sea Scrolls and Primitive Christianity* (Mentor, 1958), an attempt to clarify the connection between the Essenes and primitive Christianity; the translations are regarded as questionable by some experts.

Gaster, T. H., *Dead Sea Scriptures in English Translation* (Anchor, 1956), a judicious attempt at translating a body of texts over which furious controversies rage.

Harrison, R. K., *The Dead Sea Scrolls: An Introduction* (Harper & Row, 1961), a fairly reliable guide to the major issues regarding the nature and significance of the scrolls.

Shanks, Hershel, *Understanding the Dead Sea Scrolls* (Random House, 1992), a collection of essays from the *Biblical Archaeology Review,* providing useful access to current scholarly insights into and debates about the scrolls.

Wilson, Edmund, *Scrolls from the Dead Sea* (Meridian, 1959), still the best introduction for the novice into the obscurities of the scroll controversies.

For the general history of the period, the works cited above by Albright, Ben-Sasson, Oesterley and Robinson, and Epstein can be consulted. In addition two works of especial merit should be noted:

Bickermann, Elias, *From Ezra to the Last of the Maccabees: Foundations of Post Biblical Judaism* (Schocken, 1962), the work of a profound and original scholar.

Herford, R. T., *The Pharisees* (Beacon, 1962), a well-written, scholarly work in praise of the Pharisees.

EARLY CHRISTIANITY AND ITS ENVIRONMENT

A problem that has exercised scholars for many years is the relation of Christianity to Judaism, the extent to which Christianity can be regarded as a kind of Jewish heresy—that is, as a variation on the Jewish faith—and the extent to which it represents a completely new religious world view. Similar problems can be raised with respect to Christianity's relation to the Oriental mystery religions. The following books probe these and related problems.

Baeck, Leo, *Judaism and Christianity* (Meridian, 1961), distinguishes between two kinds of religion, classical and romantic, and defines Judaism as the former, Christianity as the latter. He stresses the "humanism" of Judaism, which requires that the individual take on responsibility for conforming to God's will, and contrasts this idea with the Christian dependence on divine aid.

Chadwick, H., *Early Christian Thought and the Classical Tradition* (Oxford University Press, 1966).

Daniel-Rops, Henri, *Jesus and His Times,* 2 vols. (Image, 1958), sets the Gospels and the events related in them into the cultural and customary life of Jesus' lifetime.

Dodd, C. H., *Old Testament in the New* (Fortress, 1963), the work of an eminent Biblical scholar, showing the continuities and the differences between the two religions.

Dodds, E. R., *Pagan and Christian in an Age of Anxiety* (Cambridge University Press, 1965; Norton, 1970).

Enslin, Martin S., *Christian Beginnings* (Harper & Row, 1956), a brilliant rehearsal for the nonspecialist of the major events in the formation of primitive Christianity as modern historical research has reconstructed them. This work deals with the political events of the last five centuries B.C., discusses the life of Jesus and the formation of the primitive church, and then summarizes current scholarship on the sources and writings of the New Testament.

Feuerbach, Ludwig, *The Essence of Christianity* (Harper & Row, 1957), an epoch-making book in religious historiography. Feuerbach was a consistent materialist, and he interpreted Christianity as another example of man's capacity for unpremeditated self-delusion, i.e., myth-making. Published in 1841, this book created a scandal, ruined Feuerbach's professional career, but set the tasks of both Christian and secularist historians of Christianity for generations to come. Well written and well translated by the English novelist George Eliot.

Fox, Robin Lane, *Pagans and Christians* (Knopf, 1987), a rich reconstruction of Christianity in the ancient pagan world.

Goodspeed, E. J., *Life of Jesus* (Harper & Row, 1956), a work by one of America's greatest New Testament scholars, carefully relating early Christian beliefs to the contemporary milieu in which they developed.

Hegel, G. W. F., *On Christianity: Early Theological Writings,* R. Kroner and T. M. Knox, eds. (Harper & Row, 1961), a selection of the great German philosopher's early reflections on the essence of Christianity. This work represents the idealist attitude against which Feuerbach was writing in his *Essence of Christianity.* Although it cannot be recommended for the reader who is not familiar with philosophy, it is a veritable treasure chest of insights into idealism.

Klausner, Joseph, *From Jesus to Paul* (Beacon, 1961), the work of one of the great Jewish scholars of the twentieth century, a sympathetic student of early Christianity, and an outstanding expert on the spiritual atmosphere in which primitive Christianity developed in Palestine.

Lebreton, Jules, and Jacques Zeiller, *History of the Early Church,* 2 vols.

(Collier, 1962), the work of two scrupulous Catholic scholars who consider the history of the early Church without regard to sectarian disputes or interests. The work is full of detailed information and is well organized.

Lietzmann, Hans, *History of the Early Church,* 2 vols. (Meridian, 1961), the Protestant equivalent of Lebreton and Zeiller; the work of a great scholar who deserves to be ranked as the successor to Adolf von Harnack. (Cf. Harnack's *The Mission and Expansion of Christianity in the First Three Centuries* [Harper & Row, 1963] and *What Is Christianity?* [Harper & Row, 1958], works that are somewhat dated now but which still provide original and informative analyses of early Christianity.)

Peters, F. E., *The Harvest of Hellenism: A History of the Near East from Alexander the Great to the Triumph of Christianity* (Simon and Schuster, 1970), a readable survey of the complex interactions of pagans, Jews, and early Christians.

————. *Judaism, Christianity, and Islam,* 3 vols. (Princeton University Press, 1990), an extensive selection of comparable passages from the classical texts of the three traditions.

Segal, Alan, *Paul the Convert: The Apostolate and Apostasy of Saul the Pharisee* (Yale University Press, 1992), argues that Paul's unique perspective of his old life as a Jew and his new life as a Christian became the basis for Christianity's misconceptions about Judaism.

THE INTERNAL DEVELOPMENT OF PRIMITIVE CHRISTIANITY

One of the most important questions in the study of primitive Christianity is the nature of Paul's contribution to the early Church: To what extent was he responsible for the form which early Christian missionary activity assumed? What was the nature of his relation to the apostles? More general questions are: How did the early Church spread and consolidate itself? To what extent did Christianity have to assume the coloration of the conventional Greek religions in order to make its message understood to potential Greek converts? What were the relations between Jew and Christian in the Diaspora? What were the relations between the Palestinian Christians and the Christians who bore no prior relation to Judaism? These and related questions are dealt with in the following works.

Cullman, Oscar, *Peter* (Meridian, 1963), a balanced and sympathetic account of the life of Peter. Cullman distinguishes carefully between that part of the tradition of Peter's life which is legend and that part which is historically plausible.

Daniel-Rops, Henri, *Church of the Apostles and Martyrs,* 2 vols. (Image, 1962), a charmingly written account of the development of the Church from the time of the Ascension to the triumph of Christianity under Theodosius the Great.

Deissmann, Adolf, *Paul: A Study in Social and Religious History* (Harper & Row, 1957), a classic work on Paul, utilizing the sociological and psychological methods of German scholarship in its golden age. Originally published in 1912.

Enslin, Martin S., *Ethics of Paul* (Apex, 1962), a circumspect and informed study.

——. *The Literature of the Christian Movement* (Harper & Row, 1956), the second volume of *Christian Beginnings,* cited above, this book deals with the literature of the New Testament in the same authoritative and engaging manner; stimulating and clear.

Goodspeed, E. J., *Twelve: The Story of Christ's Apostles* (Collier, 1962), a study of the various apostles as individuals and of the apostles as a group; utilizes non-Biblical as well as Biblical materials and shows the author's customary clarity of style and judiciousness.

Hamilton, Edith, *Witness to the Truth: Christ and His Interpreters* (Norton, 1962), an enthusiast's warm account of the life and teachings of Jesus and the various interpretations put upon them by the early Church.

Hatch, Edwin, *The Influence of Greek Ideas on Christianity* (Harper & Row, 1957), originally delivered as the Hibbert Lectures of 1888, traces the impact of Greek thought and literature on Christian ethics, rhetoric, theology, and so on. Still worth reading.

Jonas, Hans, *Gnostic Religion* (Beacon, 1963), a clear, authoritative handling of Gnostic mystical ideas; provides insights into one important aspect of the religious atmosphere within which early Christian theology made its appearance.

Meeks, Wayne A., *The First Urban Christians: The Social World of the Apostle Paul* (Yale University Press, 1983), a persuasive and fascinating explanation of the Pauline churches in their urban setting.

Nock, A. D., *Early Gentile Christianity and Its Hellenistic Background* (Harper & Row, 1964), a survey of the development of Christianity in the non-Jewish world; accurate, imaginative, and clearly written.

———. *St. Paul* (Harper & Row, 1963), the best short account of Paul in English, covering his life, his teachings, and the problems raised by any attempt to reconstruct Paul's life and work.

Schurer, E., *The History of the Jewish People in the Age of Jesus Christ* (Clark, 1973).

Schweitzer, Albert, *The Quest of the Historical Jesus* (Macmillan, 1961), surveys the attempts of scholars to reconstruct the life of Jesus throughout the nineteenth century; still the best introduction to the problem.

Toynbee, Arnold J., *Christianity among the Religions of the World* (Scribner, 1963), offers the author's usual controversial views; sets Christianity among the great religions of the world and pleads for more toleration in their study and appreciation.

Weiss, Johannes, *Earliest Christianity: A History of the Period A.D. 30–150,* 2 vols. (Harper & Row, 1959), deals with the period of the Church's first expansion in broad outline with especial attention given to the life of Paul; sees the unfolding of the Church as a tribute to Paul's genius.

CHRISTIANITY AND THE ROMAN EMPIRE

The contest between Christianity and rival sects was matched in intensity only by the contest between the increasingly triumphant Christians and the increasingly desperate Romans. At first the empire opposed Christianity, then tolerated it, and finally made it the official—and only legal—religion. What were the attitudes of early Christians toward the Roman state, and of the Roman state toward the Christians? What forms did the persecution of the early Christians take, and how did the Christians resist the persecution? What kinds of problems were raised within the Church by differing attitudes toward the political sphere? What did the pagan emperor Constantine find politically valuable in Christianity? What, in the way of intellectual and social innovations, characterized the life of the Church during the period of persecution? Finally, what sort of compromises did the Church make with the empire as the threat of persecution waned and the possibility of alliance between them increased? The following works deal with these questions.

Barnes, T. D., *Constantine and Eusebius* (Harvard University Press, 1981).

Clover, T. R., *Conflict of Religions in the Early Roman Empire* (Beacon, 1960), first published in 1909, a group of essays characterized by a firm grasp of classical thought, an appreciation of Christianity as a new religion, and an awareness of the complexity of the interrelations between the various religions of the empire.

Cochrane, Charles N., *Christianity and Classical Culture* (Galaxy, 1959), a brilliant analysis of the intellectual and ethical assumptions underlying the classical and Christian worldviews, an account of the dialogue between writers belonging to the opposed camps, and an explanation of how Christian thinkers confiscated classical ideas for the creation of a new theology. Difficult for students not already conversant with classical thought and Christian theology but without a peer in the genre.

Dawson, Christopher, *The Making of Europe* (Meridian, 1956), a study of the basic components of Western civilization as it took shape during the period of the barbarian invasions; contains brilliant chapters on the Roman Empire and the Christian Church.

Dill, Samuel, *Roman Society from Nero to Marcus Aurelius* (Meridian, 1958), a well-written study of Roman social and intellectual life, correctly assessing the strength of paganism and judiciously chronicling its failure.

Fremantle, Anne, ed., *Treasury of Early Christianity* (Mentor, 1960), carefully chosen selections from the writings of the Church Fathers, including Tertullian, Origen, Basil, and Augustine.

Frend, W. H. C., *Martyrdom and Persecution in the Early Church* (Anchor, 1967).

Jones, A. H. M., *Constantine and the Conversion of Rome* (Collier, 1962), discusses the relation between paganism and Christianity in the early empire, the breakdown of the empire in the third century A.D., and the conversion of Constantine to the Christian faith; written in a clear and straightforward manner.

MacMullen, R., *Constantine* (Harper & Row, 1971).

Marcus, R. A., *Christianity and the Roman World* (Scribner, 1974).

Segal, Alan, *Rebecca's Children: Judaism and Christianity in the Roman World* (Harvard University Press, 1986).

Simon, M., *Verus Israel. Etude sur les relations entre chrétiens et juifs dans l'Empire Romain* (Paris, 1964, 2d ed.).

Sordi, M., *The Christians and the Roman Empire* (University of Oklahoma Press, 1986).

Wardman, A., *Religion and Statecraft among the Romans* (Johns Hopkins University Press, 1982).

Wilken, Robert L., *The Christians as the Romans Saw Them* (Yale University Press, 1984), a rich reconstruction of Christianity in the ancient pagan world.

INDEX